THE SHENANDOAH VALLEY AND VIRGINIA 1861-1865

A WAR STUDY

BY

SANFORD C. KELLOGG, U. S. A.

NEW YORK & WASHINGTON

The Neale Publishing Company

COPYRIGHT, 1903, BY THE NEALE PUBLISHING COMPANY

ISBN-13: 978-1494478933

ISBN-10: 1494478935

2013 edition with notes © by Lucy Booker Roper

CONTENTS

I. The Seizure of Harper's Ferry and the Patterson Campaign 4

II. McClellan's West Virginia Campaign, including the Battle of Rich Mountain, July 11, 1861 21

III. Lewisburg, Cheat Mountain and Romney, West Virginia—Evacuation of Winchester and Manassas 30

IV. Jackson's Campaign in 1862 43

V. The Capitulation of Harper's Ferry 63

VI. Jones's and Imboden's Raid into West Virginia 77

VII. The Gettysburg Campaign and Second Battle of Winchester 115

VIII. The Averell Raids of 1863 133

IX. The Dublin Depot, New Market and Lynchburg Campaigns 157

X. The Early Raid to Washington and the Return to the Valley 157

XI. Sheridan's Campaigns—Battles of the Opequon, Fisher's Hill and Tom's Brook 178

XI. Sheridan's Campaigns (Continued)—Battle of Cedar Creek and Subsequent Cavalry Movements 202

Epilogue 224

Notes 239

CHAPTER I

THE SEIZURE OF HARPER'S FERRY AND THE PATTERSON CAMPAIGN

Virginia (which then included what is now West Virginia) seceded from the Union on the 17th of April, 1861. With the establishment of supreme sovereignty, it was only logical that Virginia authorities would occupy all formerly designated United States property within their jurisdiction, chiefly the Arsenal at Harper's Ferry. Its contents— 15,000 arms and machinery for their manufacture—was partially destroyed by fires set under command of Lieutenant Roger Jones, U. S. Army, on the night of April 18th. Lieutenant Jones then withdrew his small party to Carlisle Barracks, Pennsylvania.

The Virginia State troops occupied the Arsenal during the night of the 18th, extinguishing the fires. By the 21st of April Maj.-Gen. Kenton Harper,[i] of the Virginia State forces, reported his strength at Harper's Ferry to be "about two thousand." General Harper arranged with the Maryland State authorities for the occupation of Maryland Heights and started to Winchester with all the machinery and arms he could recover from the ruins of the Arsenal. He mentioned "the absence of all written instructions" and that he had "had to assume heavy responsibility."

This little town of Harper's Ferry, picturesquely located at the point where the Shenandoah River enters the

Potomac and where Thomas Jefferson loved to come and gaze upon the superb mountain scenery, had already, only a year and a half before, been the theater of the celebrated John Brown raid, when the Arsenal had also been seized by an irresponsible zealot as part of a wild project "to free the slaves." For this Brown and his small party paid the penalty of their lives.

To suppress the John Brown raid in October, 1859, Virginia and Maryland had recourse to their military forces. Troops were sent to the scene. Of the Virginia troops, one company of artillery, composed of cadets from the Virginia Military Institute, went from Lexington under command of the afterwards celebrated Thomas J. Jackson, who was then Professor of Applied Mathematics, Artillery Tactics, etc., at Lexington, he having resigned from the United States Army only a short while before.

The United States authorities, to repossess the Arsenal which Brown had seized and which had never been guarded, sent a party of sixty marines and other troops from Washington, all under command of Lieut.-Col. Robert E. Lee, 2d U. S. Cavalry, who had with him, as his adjutant, Lieut. J. E. B. Stuart, of the 1st Dragoons. A most interesting account of their operations is to be found in the annual report of Secretary of War J. B. Floyd, dated December 1, 1859, and in Horace Greeley's "The American Conflict," Vol. I.

With the renewed fame of Harper's Ferry as a locality in 1861, soon followed the marvelous notoriety of the principal actors in the suppression of the insane attempt of 1859, for Lieut. Col. R. E. Lee, as well as Lieut. J. E. B. Stuart, resigned from the United States Army when Virginia seceded. Lee was immediately (April 23d) appointed a major-general by Governor Letcher and assigned to command all the military and naval forces of the State; Stuart in June appears as a lieutenant-colonel of cavalry at Bunker Hill, near Winchester, while T. J. Jackson commanded a brigade[ii] nearby. All three were destined to become famous Confederate leaders.

Col. Thomas J. Jackson ("Stonewall"), on being appointed by Governor Letcher, had been ordered by General Lee, on the 27th of April, to proceed to Harper's Ferry to organize into regiments the volunteer forces collected in that vicinity, and to expedite the transfer of the machinery from the Arsenal to the Richmond Armory. He was to take command of all the forces at and near Harper's Ferry, relieving Major-General Harper.

On the 7th of May Jackson reported to Lee he had occupied and fortified Bolivar and Loudoun Heights and would do the same with Maryland Heights; that his command was badly supplied every way and that his strength should be increased to 10,000 disciplined men. He reported the Union troops as being at the Relay House, near Baltimore, on the Baltimore and Ohio Railroad. A large force was also said to be forming at Chambersburg, Pa.

On the 11th of May Jackson reported his strength at about 4,500, but not all armed. He had outposts at

Point of Rocks, Berlin, Shepherdstown and Martinsburg. He mentioned an armed Union force of Marylanders opposite Shepherdstown, threatening that place with artillery.

An order of S. Cooper, Adjutant and Inspector-General, dated Montgomery, Ala., May 15, 1861, notified Joseph E. Johnston of his appointment as brigadier-general, C. S. A., and directed him to proceed to Harper's Ferry, he having been assigned by President Davis to the command of the troops there.

At this period there was great confusion and conflict of authority arising from orders issued at Montgomery and those emanating from Richmond, in relation to military affairs in Virginia. This was partially cured by an order from Secretary of War Walker[iii] at Montgomery, dated May 10, in which General Lee, to prevent confusion, was directed to assume control of the Confederate forces in Virginia until further orders.

Later on, by the removal of the administrative machinery of the Confederate Government from Montgomery to Richmond and the absorption of the Virginia State troops into the Confederate Army, all friction was terminated.

An inspection made of the troops at Harper's Ferry and outposts on the 21st of May by Col. George Deas,[iv] mentioned the First, Second, Third, Fourth and Fifth Virginia, the Fourth Alabama, two Mississippi regiments, five companies of Virginia artillery, eight companies of Virginia cavalry, four companies of Kentucky infantry, and some small detachments, numbering in all 7,700 men, nearly all well-armed and available for active service. This force was soon afterwards increased to 20,000.

Deas reports having visited Ashby's position at Point of Rocks, twelve miles below Harper's Ferry, where he found two companies of Virginia cavalry, six pieces of light artillery, and a company of riflemen, together with some Marylanders. Ashby had control of the Baltimore and Ohio Railroad at that point with his artillery and had mined the piers of the wagon bridge over the Potomac.

Deas speaks of all the troops as raw and inexperienced; they could not well have been otherwise.

The correspondence of the Confederate authorities of this early period shows a desire to avoid as long as possible any aggressive movements, every effort being made to organize, arm and equip an effective army.

The region to the westward and northwestward of Harper's Ferry, at Berkeley (Bath), and beyond toward the Ohio River, was filled with Union men who resisted or fled from the Confederate recruiting officers. This was a great disappointment to the Richmond authorities, who counted upon getting control of the western branches of the Baltimore and Ohio Railroad, especially at Grafton and Parkersburg. It was this section that afterwards became the State of West Virginia, by refusing to accept the ordinance of secession of the mother State and by organizing a separate Statehood.

The country being mountainous, the inhabitants, like the highlanders of Kentucky, Tennessee and North Carolina, were in the main very loyal to the United States, and furnished it a valuable body of troops and scouts.

Gen. Joseph E. Johnston assumed command of the troops at Harper's Ferry on the 24th of May, pursuant to the orders of the Confederate Adjutant-General already mentioned. Colonel Jackson had not been notified of the coming of Johnston and at first demurred to yielding up the command, but when he received a communication having the endorsement "referred to Gen. J. E. Johnston, commanding officer at Harper's Ferry. By order of Major-General Lee," etc., Colonel Jackson contended no longer.

Immediately on taking command, General Johnston reported the position at Harper's Ferry untenable except by a very large force, or against an enemy strong enough to turn it above or below. His outposts extended from Williamsport through Shepherdstown to Point of Rocks, a distance of about 40 miles. General Johnston advised General Lee, that in case of a serious flank attack, the forces at Harper's Ferry and outposts be retired and employed as a screening army to oppose an enemy's advance into the lower valley, and that the troops at Harper's Ferry should never allow themselves to become invested.

General Lee, on the 31st of May, authorized General Johnston, in case he should be attacked or threatened at Harper's Ferry, to take the field and oppose the advance of an enemy into the Shenandoah Valley. However, General Lee deprecated the abandonment of Harper's Ferry on account of the depressing effect it would have upon "the cause of the South."

A column of Union troops from Ohio under General McClellan was expected by General Lee to push through eastward by the Baltimore and Ohio Railroad, to effect a junction, east of Cumberland, with the Union army forming at Chambersburg, Pa. To prevent this expected junction of the two columns, General Lee sent Gen. R. S. Garnett, early in June, 1861, to Beverly, west of the Allegheny Mountains, via Staunton, the Greenbrier country, and Huttonsville, with some organized troops and local levies, to gain possession of, or at least to obstruct, the Baltimore and Ohio Railroad between Grafton and Parkersburg. General Lee also sent a Colonel Angus MacDonald, with a light party of partisan cavalry, to break the Baltimore and Ohio Railroad at Cheat River, including roadbed, tunnels and bridges. Both of these movements were effectually prevented; General Garnett reached Huttonsville on the 14th of June, and was defeated soon after by McClellan near Beverly, while MacDonald's party never got farther than Romney.

General Lee placed so much hope in the success of the two above-mentioned raids upon the Baltimore and Ohio Railroad that he reassured General Johnston at

Harper's Ferry, on the 7th of June, as to the improbability of any immediate attack upon that position by the Federal Ohio column, and expressed the belief that General Johnston would have "merely to resist an attack in front from Pennsylvania."

Mr. Jefferson Davis was particularly averse to the evacuation of Harper's Ferry, and so expressed himself in a letter to General Beauregard at Manassas, dated June 13th, 1861, in reply to a suggestion of Beauregard that Johnston's troops might be joined to his, so that a forward aggressive movement might be made with a view to the capture of Alexandria and Arlington Heights. Mr. Davis discouraged that project with the argument that by withdrawing Johnston from the Valley of the Shenandoah, the enemy would be left free to pass to Beauregard's rear, cut his communications with Richmond and attack him in reverse, while he (Beauregard) was occupied with the enemy in his front.

On the same date, June 13th, authority to retire from Harper's Ferry, should he find it imperative to do so, was given General Johnston by Adj.-Gen. Cooper, Johnston to destroy the bridge across the Potomac and everything he could not bring off, and then to fall back on Winchester. If necessary, Johnston was to still further retire toward Manassas along the railroad from Front Royal and endeavor to check the enemy at the passes of the Blue Ridge.

On the 14th of June Johnston commenced to withdraw from Harper's Ferry, reaching Bunker Hill, 12 miles north of Winchester, on the 16th, to meet General Patterson's command of Union troops then moving from Hagerstown toward the Shenandoah Valley through Williamsport and Falling Waters.

Johnston's main force at Bunker Hill was about 7,000 strong. He had an additional force of about 5,000 under T. J. Jackson at Shepherdstown, in front of Martinsburg and along the Potomac. He also had with him a small force of cavalry under Lieut.-Col. J. E. B. Stuart, and over twenty pieces of field artillery. Winchester was then held by about 5.000 militia and some newly arrived volunteers, all covered by field works, in which twelve batteries were placed; these troops were commanded by Gen. J. H. Carson, of the Virginia State Militia.

A force of Union troops having appeared at Romney, 43 miles west of Winchester, on the 14th of June, Johnston detached three regiments under Col. A. P. Hill to meet it.

The Confederate authorities had relinquished Harper's Ferry with the greatest reluctance, principally because they still had hopes that there was sufficient disaffection in Maryland to carry that State over to the Confederacy and thus isolate Washington. These hopes had been greatly encouraged by the attack on the Sixth Massachusetts, while passing through Baltimore to Washington on the 19th of April, and the vacillating actions of the Maryland State authorities, particularly Governor Hicks, but especially by the action of both State and municipal authorities in resisting, or actually preventing, the approach of Northern troops to the relief of Washington through Baltimore or Maryland. Washington was thus isolated for three weeks.

While holding Harper's Ferry the Confederate authorities at Richmond were in actual contact with their disaffected Maryland brethren, from whom they received supplies of all kinds, besides recruits for their armies, which were openly enlisted at Baltimore by Lieut. Col. Geo. H. Steuart and others. Moreover, Harper's Ferry constituted the principal gateway for an invasion of Pennsylvania from Virginia when the time should be ripe to attempt it. It also throttled and prevented the use of the Baltimore and Ohio Railroad by the Federal authorities as a means of communication east and west.

It was as important a point on their northern frontier for the Confederates to hold as Chattanooga afterwards became on their central line. Consequently, the troops guarding that important gateway were strengthened as rapidly as circumstances would permit, Johnston's army being justly regarded as second only in importance to that of Beauregard at Manassas, then threatening Washington.

The Capital's position during May and June, 1861 was critical, the enemy's lines and outposts being advanced almost to the fortifications; the enemy's left flank extended to Leesburg, with pickets along the Potomac from the Chain Bridge to Point of Rocks, threatening to cross at the many fords and ferries.

General McDowell was placed in command of the troops in front of Washington on the 27th of May, the aged General Winfield Scott retaining the direction of all the armies in the field.

Communication with the North through Baltimore had then been effectually restored by Gen. B. F. Butler, who seized that city by a coup de main on May 14th, 1861, the citizens finding him in possession of Federal Hill when they opened their windows that morning. Their surprise was equaled only by that of General Scott and the Washington authorities, who had given no orders for the movement; on the contrary, General Scott so much disapproved of General Butler's action that he relieved him from the command the following day and sent him to Fortress Monroe. Reinforcements for Washington were then rushed through Baltimore even to the extent of weakening Patterson's column, then assembling at Chambersburg to operate toward Harper's Ferry and Cumberland.

A column of about 2,500 men under General Stone was organized at Washington on the 8th of June to proceed through Rockville, Maryland, toward Edward's Ferry on the Potomac and Leesburg in Virginia, as a diversion in favor of Patterson's expected advance on Harper's Ferry from Chambersburg. Stone made his headquarters at Poolesville and eventually extended his pickets to the Monocacy River and Noland's Ferry. He did not connect with Patterson's troops and had nothing on his right.

Another diversion in Patterson's favor was made from the center of McDowell's army as far as Vienna, Va., on the 17th of June, toward Leesburg, but which threatened to become so serious an affair and caused General Scott such uneasiness that he stopped General Patterson's movement south of the Potomac at Williamsport, ordered him to re-cross the river, and detached from him all his most experienced troops and all his artillery, for service at Washington. This left Patterson with a force composed almost entirely of three-months' men and no artillery capable of being moved for lack of horses.

McClellan's operations in West Virginia, from which so much assistance to Patterson's movement on Harper's Ferry had been expected, failed of realization, although McClellan did succeed in reopening and firmly holding the Baltimore and Ohio Railroad as far eastward as Cumberland, to which point he pushed Col. Lew Wallace's Eleventh Indiana Regiment, but could not afterwards spare any other troops to support the position, as all of McClellan's then available force was being used in keeping open and securing the railroad west of Cumberland, besides operating against the troops of Garnett south of the railroad at Philippi, Buckhannon, Beverly, and Rich Mountain, where McClellan finally defeated Garnett and dispersed his command on the 11th of July and occupied Beverly on the 12th.

This was a beautiful strategic movement of two converging columns—one from Buckhannon and the other from Philippi—on the enemy's two strong positions at Rich Mountain and Laurel Hill, covering Beverly, and resulted in the loss to the enemy of all his stores and artillery, a great part of his wagons, with 135 killed, and over 800 prisoners, of whom a large number were wounded.

Wallace, who reached Cumberland on the 11th of June and communicated with Patterson, made a reconnaissance southeastward toward Winchester, which reached Romney on the 14th, where he attacked and dispersed MacDonald's forces strengthened by two pieces of artillery, after which Wallace returned to Cumberland. This was the Federal force mentioned by Johnston and against which he detached Hill with three regiments. Wallace's movement proved serviceable to Patterson, as it alarmed the militia and other troops at Winchester and attracted the attention of Johnston and Jackson at Bunker Hill and Martinsburg, who believed Wallace's forces to be the advance of McClellan's West Virginia column.

Wallace at Cumberland then became uneasy because of rumors (which afterwards proved unfounded) that he was to be attacked by a heavy force from the west and south. He called on General Patterson, who had not then crossed the Potomac, for assistance. Patterson instructed Wallace to move toward Hancock, eastward, or, if that was not feasible, to retire northward into Bedford, Pa., unless he could hold his own at Cumberland. Patterson detached Burnside's newly-arrived Rhode Island regiment and battery, on the

16th, to move to meet Wallace at Hancock; but Burnside was almost immediately recalled by orders from Washington and sent to the latter point, together with all the regular troops and all the artillery forming a part of Patterson's column, to meet a threatened attack on the Capital.

With the bulk of the remainder of his army, then reduced to barely 12,000 men, Patterson crossed the Potomac at Williamsport on the 16th of June and advanced to find the enemy; but the same orders which called away the Rhode Island Regiment and all the regular troops, directed Patterson to re-cross the Potomac, which he did on the 17th and 18th, but not before he had driven the enemy southward through Martinsburg and also beyond Falling Waters. Johnston, with 12,000 men, then reoccupied Martinsburg and threatened to cross at Williamsport, which had the effect of delaying the sending off of the troops ordered to Washington, so that they did not all go until the 21st of June.

The aggressive movement into the Shenandoah Valley was thus abandoned for the time being. Patterson established himself in front of Harper's Ferry, at Williamsport, Falling Waters and Sharpsburg, his own headquarters being at Hagerstown. He was called upon by General Scott to project a new campaign, but to remain in front of Johnston's army. After persistent solicitation, Patterson succeeded in obtaining the Rhode Island battery once more, and Stone's Brigade of three regiments and a half from Poolesville; he also got the harness he needed to move his only battery (Perkins's), so that on the 2d of July, with about 10,000 men, he re-crossed the Potomac into Virginia near Falling Waters and forced back T. J. Jackson's force of about 4,000 infantry, artillery and cavalry to beyond Martinsburg, which Patterson occupied again on the 3d of July and halted for supplies. Part of Stone's command joined Patterson there on the 8th of July, when preparations were at once made to move on Winchester, in which direction all of Johnston's army had retired, but finding several of his officers unfavorable to that movement, Patterson called a council of war on the 9th, at which it was decided to remain in observation of Johnston, but not to pursue him, as it was known he had been heavily reinforced, some extravagant estimates of Johnston's strength at Winchester being 40,000 men of all arms.

On the 15th of July Patterson moved his army to Bunker Hill, and on the 17th to Charlestown; his base was then established at Harper's Ferry, ten miles away. The terms of service of his three-months' men commenced to expire and but very few would consent to remain longer.

McDowell commenced his advance from Washington toward Manassas on the 18th of July via Fairfax Court House. Naturally, great anxiety was felt as to the effect this movement would have upon Johnston's army in the Shenandoah. Patterson's instructions were to endeavor to detain Johnston, but if he went towards Manassas, Patterson was to cross the Shenandoah

River near its mouth at Keyes's Ferry and march to McDowell's assistance via Hillsboro and Leesburg. Johnston did get away from Winchester without the knowledge of Patterson on the 18th (the same day that McDowell passed through Fairfax Court-House), and marched via Millwood and Ashby's Gap to Piedmont on the Manassas Gap Railway during the 19th and 20th, the last of his entire force arriving upon the Bull Run Battlefield during the 21st, his advance guard under Jackson reaching Manassas as early as 4 p. M. of the 19th.

Had McDowell's attack been hastened by but two days, Johnston could not have reached Beauregard in time to assist him. As it was he brought with him a reinforcement of over 10,000 men. Patterson was too weak to have prevented him from going, even if he had known of Johnston's departure; and he was too deficient in wagon transportation to have reached McDowell before Johnston could get to Beauregard, particularly as he (Patterson) would be on an exterior line.

After the Battle of Bull Run Major-General Banks was sent from Baltimore to relieve Patterson at Harper's Ferry, reaching there July 25; Major-General McClellan was called from West Virginia to command the Division of the Potomac, superseding General McDowell, and assumed that command also on the 25th of July.

The original order for Patterson's relief was dated July 19, before the Battle of Bull Run, to take effect July 27, "when his tour of duty will expire." The same order designated the Valley of Virginia as the future Department of the Shenandoah (G O. 46, of 1861). Patterson held the commission of major-general of Pennsylvania militia, which had been ordered out for three months' service in the field under the call of the President the day after the firing on Fort Sumter, April 14, 1861.

CHAPTER II

M'Clellan's West Virginia Campaign, Including the Battle of Rich Mountain, July 11, 1861.

With a small advance party General McClellan personally reached Grafton by rail from Ohio on the 23rd of June, his column consisting of seven regiments, three batteries, and one troop of cavalry closely following. Grafton had been occupied from Wheeling as early as May 30 by Col. B. F. Kelley, First Virginia Volunteers, supported by Col. J. Irvine's Sixteenth Ohio. The Fourteenth Ohio, Col. J. B. Steedman, was sent at the same time from Marietta, Ohio, to occupy Parkersburg. Colonel Kelley then moved on Philippi, fifteen miles south of Grafton, where a Confederate force several hundred strong, under Col. George A. Porterfield, had collected. This latter force had been operating on the Baltimore and Ohio Railroad north and west of Grafton, burning bridges, etc. Colonel Kelley received his orders from Gen. T. A. Morris, Indiana Volunteers, who had reached Grafton with four Indiana regiments from Indianapolis on the 1st of June, and assumed command.

On the 2d of June two cooperating columns were sent by General Morris to Philippi; one, under Kelley, went by rail to a point 6 miles east of Grafton, and then, by a delayed night march, to Philippi; the other column, under Colonel Dumont, of the Seventh Indiana, went by rail to Webster, a few miles from Grafton, and then marched in the same direction as Kelley's column, but by a different route, both columns timing the movement so as to reach the vicinity of Philippi very early on the morning of June 3d, Dumont to attract attention from Kelley's movements. The two columns reached Philippi almost simultaneously, surprising and routing the enemy, who was pursued in the direction of Beverly and Huttonsville, where Colonel Porterfield met reinforcements, and remained in command until superseded, on the 14th of June, by Gen. R. S. Garnett, especially sent from Richmond by General Lee.

Immediately on assuming command of the Confederate troops at Huttonsville, General Garnett moved them northward through Beverly, where he established his depot, to the passes of the mountains westward through Rich Mountain on the Buckhannon road and northward on the Philippi road at Laurel Hill. Both positions were then fortified and some few pieces of artillery placed in the fortifications. He had an outpost at Leadsville, on the St. George road, to protect his rear.

General Garnett's instructions from General Lee were not only to impede McClellan's advance eastward through the passes, but also to endeavor to break the Baltimore and Ohio Railroad effectually by destroying the Cheat River viaduct. The latter part of these orders Garnett was never able to accomplish, but to secure his own position in and about Beverly he blocked all the mountain roads in the direction of the enemy as far north as St. George, the county seat of Tucker County. He found the Union sentiment strongly in the ascendency among the people of the country, and complained to General Lee that he neither could get assistance from them nor prevent their giving information to the enemy of all his movements. His strength was about 10,000 men, with six pieces of artillery, as shown by his ration returns, when McClellan attacked him on the 11th of July at Rich Mountain; but he had made the fatal mistake of dividing his force, although both of his main positions at Rich Mountain and at Laurel Hill were strong.

After securing the position at Philippi with Morris's Brigade, and placing a force of 2,000 men at Cheat River Bridge and Rowlesburg under Brig.-Gen. C. W. Hill, ample forces were kept by McClellan at Grafton, Webster, Clarksburg and Parkersburg to maintain rail communication with Ohio. With the surplus regiments reaching him from Ohio and Indiana, McClellan organized at Buckhannon a column of about 6,000 men to attack Garnett, with the expectation of driving him out toward Staunton.

While McClellan attacked Garnett in front at Rich Mountain, Morris, with the forces at Philippi (about 6,000), was to move to Laurel Hill and capture that position if Garnett evacuated or weakened it.

McClellan's column was organized into two brigades under Rosecrans and Schleich. Early on the morning of July n he sent Rosecrans with 2,000 men through the mountains south of the enemy's fortified position, by a circuitous route, which brought Rosecrans at noon into the turnpike, two or three miles to the enemy's rear, on the crest of Rich Mountain at Hart's Farm. With the other troops and twelve guns, McClellan moved directly on the fortified camp at the foot of Rich Mountain near Roaring Creek, but before McClellan attacked it Rosecrans's flank movement had forced its abandonment.

Rosecrans had met with no resistance until he reached Hart's Farm, on the turnpike on top of the mountain, where the only casualties to McClellan's column occurred and these were but slight—only 12 killed and 49 wounded; whereas, the enemy's loss, there and in the pursuit which followed, was 135 killed and. 800 prisoners, including among the latter Lieutenant-Colonel Pegram, the commanding officer on that part of the line, who first endeavored to escape, but then surrendered with a party of 593, including 33 officers. The remainder of the enemy's force was dispersed and pursued towards Huttonsville and Monterey southeastward through Beverly, which latter place, with all its stores, was captured on the 12th. McClellan pursued only as far as Cheat Mountain.

While the attack on Rich Mountain was progressing, Garnett, with the remainder of his troops, was at Laurel Hill, confronted by the Philippi troops under Morris. The distance from Beverly to Laurel Hill is 17 miles, and from Beverly to the fortified camp at the foot of Rich Mountain, 7 miles.

When Garnett found the enemy bad gained his rear and his communications southward toward Staunton, he evacuated Laurel Hill, abandoned his camp equipage, and retreated northward through Leadsville to Cheat River, Morris following him with part of his force, but not with sufficient vigor to complete his destruction. Three of Morris's regiments and Barnett's Battery came up with the enemy, however, and engaged him in a spirited action at Carrick's Ford of Cheat River, 8 miles south of St. George. In this affair—a rearguard action—Garnett was killed and many of his wagons captured. This part of the pursuit was then halted, 26 miles from Laurel Mountain, on the 13th instant.

As soon as General McClellan occupied Beverly, early on the 12th, and he ascertained that Garnett's main force was retreating northward through the mountains, he ordered General Hill, on the railroad,—at Grafton and Rowlesburg,—to collect a force of 5,000 men and endeavor to head off the enemy toward St. George and eastward on the Northwestern turnpike. Hill had an outpost on that road at West Union, 13 miles east of Rowlesburg. An additional force of 500 men on the 12th had reached the Red House, 8 miles still farther east on the Northwestern turnpike, via Oakland, on the railroad, and Chisholm's Mill, but through error had then gone on westward to join the troops at West Union instead of pushing out southward toward St. George.

Although Hill had reached Oakland on the night of the 13th by rail and hurriedly moved out 12 miles to the Red House with such of his forces as had arrived, they were entirely lacking in wagon transportation, and could accomplish nothing beyond following the remnant of Garnett's army, which had already passed the Red House early on the 14th, avoiding West Union, and was moving southward on the Northwestern turnpike toward Petersburg, West Virginia, Franklin and Monterey, in the valley of the South Fork of the Potomac. The few cavalry sent by Hill to try to take contact with the retreating enemy went as far as

Stoney Creek and then turned back, having only seen a few stragglers in the distance.

Another effort, with a stronger force, was made on the 15th by Hill to come up with the enemy toward Petersburg. This party went almost to Petersburg on the 17th, when it was recalled by a dispatch from McClellan to discontinue the pursuit.

While McClellan's operations from Buckhannon and Philippi were proceeding, contemporaneously with Patterson's movement near Harper's Ferry, Gen. J. D. Cox, with five regiments, was ordered by McClellan from Ohio, into the Kanawha Valley, early in July, to clear that region of any enemy and to act as a collateral column to his own movements against Garnett.

Cox's opponent in the Kanawha was Gen. Henry A. Wise, with a force estimated at about 3,000 badly- organized men, known as the Wise Legion. In an engagement which took place at Scarey Creek, July 16, between Wise and Cox, the latter was defeated (very much to McClellan's disgust) and his advance checked until he could get reinforcements from Ohio, when he moved on again up the Kanawha, forcing Wise back beyond Charleston and the Gauley, Wise finally retreating to Lewisburg, August 1st, his movements being hastened by the threatening position of some of Rosecrans's troops at Weston and Summerville, on his right flank and rear.

The news of Cox's repulse at Scarey Creek, following upon Morris's dilatory pursuit of Garnett's forces on Pleasant Run and Cheat River, to which was added the fact that Garnett's retreating command had passed across the front of Hill's troops at the Red House, unmolested, caused McClellan intense disappointment.

The results of these movements, however, were the chasing out of the enemy from the western slope of the Alleghenies in West Virginia and the freeing of the Kanawha as high up as the Gauley, besides the securing of the Baltimore and Ohio Railroad from Parkersburg and Wheeling eastward to Cumberland. McClellan was then called east and Rosecrans succeeded to the command.

The locations of the armies in Virginia (including West Virginia) August 1, 1861, were as follows:

Rosecrans, commanding McClellan's old army, holding Gauley Bridge, Summerville, Beverly and Cheat

Mountain; Garnett's Confederate army dispersed toward Staunton, but its remnants being collected at Monterey by Gen. W. W. Loring, strengthened by ten regiments and two batteries, with outposts at Elk and Middle Mountains and the crest of the Alleghenies, drawing its supplies from Staunton by way of Millboro.

Wise's Confederate Legion was at Lewisburg, where Floyd was marching with troops from Dublin Depot on the Virginia and Tennessee Railroad to join him. Banks at Harper's Ferry, commanding Patterson's old army, with no enemy of consequence to confront him nearer than Winchester.

McClellan at Washington, commanding the army that recently had been defeated at Bull Run under McDowell, and which was still closely threatened from the direction of Manassas by the enemy under Beauregard and Johnston.

Butler at Fortress Monroe, the Rip Raps, and Newport News, with several thousand men, unable to make any headway up the Peninsula against Magruder at Yorktown.

Norfolk and the Navy Yard were strongly held by the Confederates, while the Virginia and East Tennessee Railroad was not yet within striking distance of any Federal army.

General Scott still retained direction of all the Union armies, although it was beginning to be recognized he was past the age for active, efficient service.

It may not be amiss here to remark that Generals R. E. Lee, McDowell, and McClellan had all three been especial favorites of General Scott when the war commenced in April, 1861, and also that General Scott was somewhat inclined to permit the "wayward sisters [to] depart in peace."

CHAPTER III
LEWISBURG, CHEAT MOUNTAIN AND ROMNEY,
WEST VIRGINIA EVACUATION OF WINCHESTER AND MANASSAS

On the 1st of September, 1861, Gen. J. E. Johnston, who remained in command of the Confederate army at Manassas after the Battle of Bull Run, recommended the reduction of Carson's Militia at Winchester to 2,500 men, as Banks had shown no disposition to advance from Harper's Ferry, and as all surplus men were needed to cultivate the Valley, where the percentage of slaves was very small. Considerable local agitation on the subject of getting the services of as many men as possible for agricultural purposes had existed for some weeks, culminating in strong appeals to Richmond from such local magnates as Randolph Tucker *et al.*

McClellan's army, as well as Banks's, remained strictly on the defensive throughout the summer and autumn of 1861 and until March, 1862, with the exception of an occasional reconnaissance and consequent skirmish. The enemy was not prevented from obstructing the Potomac below Washington with batteries, notably at Evansport and at Matthias's Point, threatening to sever communication by water with Fortress Monroe.

A serious engagement with the enemy on the 21st of October at Ball's Bluff,[v] near Leesburg, had resulted in a disaster to the Federal troops before they could be withdrawn.

The only activity was in West Virginia, where General Lee had gone in person to take command of the Confederates, after Garnett's defeat near Beverly and Wise's retreat eastward from the Kanawha to Lewisburg. Lee called to Wise's assistance from the East Tennessee and Virginia Railroad a column of about 4,000 men under Gen. J. B. Floyd (the former Secretary of War of the United States), which force marched northward through the valley of New River and then joined Wise at Lewisburg. This joint force of about 6,000 men under Floyd was then moved by General Lee back toward the Gauley, to endeavor to regain the territory lost by Wise, but found the position at Gauley Bridge too strongly held by Cox to justify attacking it. Besides, a movement of Rosecrans's force from Summerville towards Floyd's right flank at Carnifix Ferry, on the Gauley, diverted Floyd in that direction, resulting in Floyd being forced to retreat by Rosecrans at the last-named place on the 10th of September. By this affair Rosecrans preserved his communications with Cox lower down on the Gauley at its junction with New River, and Rosecrans, with Cox, then turned his attention toward breaking the enemy's rail communications between Virginia and Tennessee at New River Bridge, by sending an expedition to Raleigh Court-House and beyond, which, however, never succeeded in getting farther than Princeton or in reaching the railroad, although Floyd, in November, again retreated from before Rosecrans toward the railroad.

Before going to direct the movements at Lewisburg, General Lee had assumed charge of the Confederate forces in the Allegheny Mountains at Monterey and Huntersville, commanded by Generals H. R. Jackson and Loring. With these, on the 12th of September, he made a strong reconnaissance of the Federal positions on Cheat Mountain and toward Huttonsville, and, having satisfied himself of their strength, he then turned his attention to Lewisburg.

While these movements were progressing, considerable activity was being shown by the Federal forces on the line of the Baltimore and Ohio Railroad from about Cumberland toward Winchester.

On the 24th of October Gen. B. F. Kelley, at Cumberland, under orders from Gen. Winfield Scott, formed an expedition of about twenty-two companies of infantry, a troop of cavalry, and two guns, at New Creek (now called Keyser, but shown on the maps as Paddytown), on the Baltimore and Ohio Railroad, to operate on Romney, 26 miles southeast. This force left New Creek at midnight of the 25th, and marched through Mechanicsburg Gap to within three miles of Romney without opposition. A supporting column from Patterson's Creek, consisting of the Second Maryland Infantry (Colonel Johns), also moved southward through Frankfort and Springfield toward Romney, but was met by the enemy at a bridge over the

South Branch of the Potomac about eight miles from Romney, and there checked on the 26th. With his own column, however, General Kelley captured Romney after some resistance and pursued the enemy under Colonel MacDonald through and beyond the town, on the Winchester pike, capturing all his trains and artillery, camp equipage, etc. General Kelley then occupied Romney, where he remained until January, when he was threatened by Jackson in force, and retired again toward New Creek Station.

This occupation of Romney and the driving out of MacDonald's Confederates had created much uneasiness at Winchester and in the army at Manassas, as it was again supposed to be the advance of the Federal troops from West Virginia endeavoring to form a junction with Banks, just as, earlier, in June, a similar movement on Romney by Wallace had been believed to be the advance of McClellan's West Virginia forces to cooperate with Patterson. This uneasiness resulted in the sending of Gen. T. J. Jackson, on the 1st of November, from the Manassas army to take charge of the operations about Winchester and in the northern part of the Shenandoah Valley.

Jackson first called out all the local militia belonging to Boggs's, Carson's and Meem's Brigades, many of these men having gone to their homes to attend to their farms, etc. He then was joined during November by his old brigade, composed of the Second, Fourth, Fifth, Twenty-seventh and Thirty-third Virginia Volunteers, and, during December, by Taliaferro's Brigade and Loring's Division, which had been withdrawn via Staunton from about Monterey and Huntersville, in the Allegheny Mountains, where it had been found impracticable to maintain and supply them in winter quarters.

This reinforcement gave Jackson, besides the militia, sixteen regiments of infantry and three batteries of fairly well-seasoned artillery. He also had a respectable force of cavalry under Cols. Turner Ashby and Angus MacDonald (a partisan ranger). Banks still continued north of the Potomac at Harper's Ferry, with his flanks extended to cover Williamsport and Point of Rocks.

Jackson first turned his attention to disabling the Chesapeake and Ohio Canal, which follows the north shore of the Potomac, and did succeed in breaking Dam No. 5 near Williamsport, on the 21st of December, but not irreparably.

On the 1st of January, 1862, Jackson, with about 8,500 men, moved from the vicinity of Winchester northward toward Bath (Berkeley Springs), which was taken on the 4th, the small party of Federal infantry and cavalry holding it retreating six miles to Hancock. Two regiments and a battery were sent by Jackson to destroy the railroad bridge over the Big Cacapon River. A brigade under Colonel Gilham was detached at Bath to pursue the Federals in the direction of Sir John's Run, a station on the Baltimore and Ohio Railroad east of Hancock, but did not come up with them. However, the next day, January 5th, the entire force proceeded to destroy the railroad below and opposite Hancock, the Federals in that town, which is on the north bank of the Potomac, refusing to surrender, while the party sent to Cacapon Bridge accomplished its destruction. Jackson says that "on the 6th the enemy [at Hancock] was reinforced to such an extent as to induce me to believe that my object could not be accomplished without a sacrifice of life, which I felt unwilling to make; as Romney, the great object of the expedition, might require for its recovery, and especially for the capture of the troops in and near there, all the force at my disposal."

So, on the 7th of January, Jackson, with his entire force of over 8,000 men, moved toward Romney, via Unger's Store, at which latter place he halted "for several days;" but the Federal forces evacuated Romney on the 10th and fell back to the railroad west of Patterson's Creek.

Loring's Division was then placed by Jackson in winter quarters at Romney, and the local militia sent to the vicinity of their homes, not far away. By extending southward up the South Branch of the Potomac, via Moorefield, connection was made with Gen. Edward Johnson's Brigade at Monterey, and the entire region secured against immediate attack from west of the Alleghenies.

Carson's Brigade of Militia was posted at Bath and Meem's Brigade of Militia at Martinsburg, while Jackson took his old brigade (now commanded by Gen. R. B. Garnett) back with him to Winchester as a reserve.

Then arose one of those situations which the lack of discipline of the troops and the intermeddling of politicians often causes discontent to self-respecting commanding generals. In this case it caused Jackson to tender his "conditional resignation," because the Acting Confederate Secretary of War (Benjamin) ordered Jackson to withdraw Loring's command from Romney and the South Branch of the Potomac, giving as a reason that they were informed at Richmond a movement by the Federals was being made to cut Loring off. The true reason was that Loring's officers and Loring himself did not fancy being kept at Romney when they might be more comfortable and enjoy the social advantages of Winchester, only forty-three miles away, during the remainder of the winter. Hence their appeal to Richmond over Jackson's head.

It required all the influence of Gen. Joseph E. Johnston, Governor Letcher and many of Jackson's brother officers to induce him finally to withdraw his resignation. His forebodings as to the result of withdrawing Loring from Romney proved true, for that place and Moorefield were almost immediately reoccupied by Kelley's command, the Federal outposts being advanced on the 14th of February to Bloomery Pass, within twenty-one miles of Winchester, capturing there, after considerable resistance, sixty-five officers and privates of Sencendiver's (Carson's) Brigade. From Bloomery a dash was also made to Unger's Store.

General Banks, whose headquarters were established at Frederick, Md., held the line of the upper Potomac from Hancock to Berlin. On the 25th of February a detachment of fourteen companies of infantry, a squadron of the First Michigan Cavalry, and four guns was sent, under Col. John W. Geary, Twenty-eighth Pennsylvania, across the river at Harper's Ferry and then across the Shenandoah River and Loudoun Heights into Pleasant Valley eastward, small parties of Confederates retiring before Geary through Lovettsville and Waterford toward Leesburg, which place was occupied by Colonel Geary at sunrise of March 8th, the Confederate forces under D. H. Hill retreating southward through Middleburg. On the 12th Geary marched to Snickersville, after leaving a small garrison at Leesburg, and thence to Upperville on the 15th, reconnoitering en route the gaps of the Blue Ridge and Front Royal, finally halting at Aldie on the 24th of March, having cleared Loudoun County of the enemy. Johnston's army was then withdrawing from the Manassas line.

The remainder of A. S. Williams's Brigade, to which Geary belonged, had advanced on the 4th of March from Williamsport through Martinsburg to Bunker Hill. Shields's Brigade followed Williams's.'

On the 9th of March, 1862, Johnston's army fell back from Centerville, Manassas and Dumfries to the line of the Rappahannock, the movement being evidently hastily made, as the valuable guns in the works at Cockpit Point and Evansport, on the Potomac, were abandoned; 800 barrels of flour were destroyed at Dumfries, besides a great quantity of general stores at Manassas. Gordonsville was then made the Confederate depot for supplies. This retrograde movement was a great surprise to the Richmond authorities, as it was not ordered from there, although preparations for it had been made.

The retirement of Johnston's army was closely followed up by the advance of McClellan's, Centerville being occupied by Kearney's Brigade on the 10th and Manassas by the Third and Eighth Pennsylvania Cavalry on the 14th. Repairs to the Manassas Gap Railroad and the railroad back to Alexandria were commenced at once, under the direction of Col. D. C. McCallum.

Johnston's withdrawal from Manassas and Banks' advance on Winchester caused Jackson to retire on Strasburg, which he accomplished on the 13th of March, Banks occupying Winchester on that same date. Shields's Division of 11,000 men, on the 19th, advanced to Strasburg, 18 miles, Jackson retiring to Woodstock and thence to Mount Jackson, 23 miles farther up the Valley, where he had previously established his depot.

Williams's Division of Banks's Corps had been ordered to Washington, via Harper's Ferry, thus leaving Shields alone in the Valley.

On the 13th of March, 1862, Gen. R. E. Lee was placed by executive orders in command of all the armies of the Confederacy, with his headquarters "at the seat of government." This gave General Lee the same general authority over the Confederates for combined movements as was conferred upon General McClellan when he relieved General Scott on the 1st of November, 1861, of the command of all the armies of the United States.

McClellan had been busy all the autumn and winter of 1861 reorganizing the Army of the Potomac and supervising the campaigns of all the other armies then in the field, but he gave his principal attention to the army at Washington and to its preparation for an offensive campaign as soon as the roads in Virginia would admit, or the general preparedness of his army would justify a forward movement. The deliberative delay of McClellan in dealing with these problems caused so much impatient agitation by the newspaper press of the country, that the Government was compelled to urge McClellan to perfect his plans and move the Army of the Potomac aggressively upon the enemy. The strength of Johnston's army when at Centerville, Manassas and Dumfries was greatly overestimated as being 100,000 strong, whereas, Johnston never had more than 50,000 present, as his returns for February show, while McClellan on the same date had assembled at and in front of Washington a force of 222,000 "present and absent."

In announcing to the President his general plan for the movement of the Army of the Potomac, McClellan favored a scheme to avoid attacking Johnston's army and to move the bulk of his force by water down the Potomac into Chesapeake Bay, thence up the Rappahannock River to Urbana, making that a sub-base for attacking Richmond, via West Point, only three marches distant from Urbana. A large force was to be left at Washington to secure it beyond hazard. The movement to the Chesapeake and thence toward Richmond by river was predicated upon using Fortress Monroe as the main base, having the cooperation of the navy in the rivers and on the bay, getting into a country where campaigning was more favorable than in Northern Virginia in winter. This plan was afterwards changed to a movement up the Peninsula between the York and James Rivers to West Point and Richmond.

On the 31st of January the President had ordered "that all the disposable force of the Army of the Potomac, after providing safely for the defense of Washington, be formed into an expedition for the immediate object of seizing and occupying a point on the railroad southwestward of what is known as Manassas Junction, the expedition to move on or before the 22d of February next"; and while he disapproved McClellan's project of an expedition to attack Richmond by way of Chesapeake Bay, he did not insist subsequently on the above order to move on the 22d of February being immediately executed, for means of transportation by water were being accumulated and other arrangements for the proposed Chesapeake Bay expedition, attention meanwhile being given to reopening the Baltimore and Ohio Railroad from Cumberland eastward, to do which it became necessary to throw Banks's command across the Potomac, force the evacuation of Martinsburg, and drive the enemy well up toward Winchester and Strasburg.

This heavy flanking movement, which has already been described, and McClellan's large army in front, caused first the withdrawal of the enemy from Leesburg, then Winchester, and finally Manassas and Centerville, including the abandonment of the batteries which had impeded the navigation of the Potomac.

On the same day that the enemy was withdrawing from Manassas and Winchester, March 9, 1862, there occurred in Hampton Roads the celebrated defeat of the Merrimac by the Monitor, and as there no longer existed any serious obstacle to the carrying out of McClellan's Chesapeake Bay project, the President consented to its execution after McClellan had pursued Johnston's retreating army as rapidly as the terrible roads permitted, and had definitely located it in its new position beyond the Rappahannock, and near the Orange and Alexandria Railroad. McClellan then embarked at Alexandria the troops constituting the Peninsula expedition, the vanguard leaving there on the 1st of April.

General McClellan having taken the field with the Army of the Potomac, the President temporarily rearranged the other commands by placing Major-General Halleck in command of the armies operating in Kentucky, Tennessee and Missouri, designating that section as the Department of the Mississippi; the army operating west of the Shenandoah and east of Halleck's armies, in West Virginia principally, constituted the Mountain Department, under Maj.-Gen. John C. Fremont.

After McClellan's departure for his Peninsula campaign, separate commands were made of the army left in front of Washington under McDowell and the force under Banks left to guard the northern part of the Shenandoah Valley (at Strasburg and toward Front Royal, on the Manassas Gap Railroad), for Stonewall Jackson, with 6,500 men, still showed great activity in the Valley from near Mount Jackson. The separate commanders reported direct to the Secretary of War.

Shields, who had followed Jackson on the 19th of March in the direction of Mount Jackson, first fell back to Strasburg and then, on the 20th, to Winchester, Shields says, "to draw him [Jackson] from his position and supporting force, if possible." In that Shields succeeded, for Jackson followed him and attacked him on the 22d and 23d near Kernstown, immediately south of Winchester, with the result that Jackson was badly beaten, losing 80 killed, 375 wounded, 270 missing and two guns, besides being forced to return again to Mount Jackson. Shields' own loss was 118 killed, 450 wounded and 22 missing.

———

CHAPTER IV
Jackson's Campaign Of 1862

Two brigades of Williams's Division of Banks's Corps, that had already started on their march to Manassas, were recalled from Castleman's Ferry, of the Shenandoah, to assist Shields, but did not reach Winchester until the 24th, after the Battle of Kernstown; they took part, however, in the pursuit of Jackson as far as Strasburg.

On the 1st of April Banks, with five brigades (less the necessary garrisons left at strategic points and as guards at bridges, etc.), advanced from Strasburg, 18 miles, to Edenburg, the enemy contesting his movement. At Edenburg a halt for 15 days was made to bring forward supplies, scant wagon transportation being given as the reason for the delay there. On the 17th of April another forward movement up the Valley turnpike was made through Mount Jackson to New Market, the latter place being twelve miles south of Edenburg. There Banks held his main body and established his headquarters temporarily, sending out his cavalry and some of his infantry to seize and hold Columbia Bridge over the Shenandoah, 12 miles eastward on the Luray road. Another and a larger party of cavalry and infantry went 17 miles farther south, to Harrisonburg, on the 24th of April, where another halt was made to bring up supplies. At Harrisonburg Banks was within 25 miles of Staunton.

Jackson had left Harrisonburg on the 19th of April and marched eastward 18 miles into Elk Run Valley, at Conrad's Store, east of the Shenandoah and at the foot of Swift Run Gap, in the Blue Ridge. In his new position Jackson was near support from Gordonsville and Culpeper, via Stannardsville or Madison Court House, which could come to him either through Swift Run Gap or one 17 miles farther north. This support had been provided by General Lee, and consisted of Ewell's Division, 8,000 strong, which was marched from Culpeper toward Jackson and joined him west of the Blue Ridge, on the 30th of April, by way of Swift Run Gap.

McClellan's movement to the Peninsula had required the reinforcement of Magruder's forces at Yorktown early in April, resulting in the withdrawal of Johnston's army toward Richmond from Central Virginia, except a body of 2,500 men left at Fredericksburg (which later also withdrew) and a force of 8,000 under Ewell at Culpeper to observe the Federals at Warrenton, as well as defend the line of the Rapidan.

Jackson entertained the hope that Banks might move toward Staunton, when it was his purpose to dash suddenly from Elk River Valley (Swift Run Gap) through the Massanutten Range, attack Banks in rear and sever his communication with Strasburg and Winchester; but Banks's orders from McClellan were to proceed only to New Market and Harrisonburg with his main army, so Banks was not to be lured any farther south. Another column of Federals, under Milroy[vi] from west of the Alleghenies was, however, threatening Staunton from the direction of Monterey, the Confederates under Gen. Edward Johnson, who had been holding Monterey, having been obliged to fall back to Buffalo Gap, near Staunton, before Milroy's advance; Milroy reached McDowell in the Bull Pasture Valley[vii] on the 20th of April. He was then 26 miles from Staunton, on the Parkersburg turnpike, where it crosses Shenandoah Mountain.

Gen. R. C. Schenck's Brigade of Fremont's army (to which Milroy also belonged) was moving up the South Branch of the Potomac from Romney through Moorefield to Franklin, keeping parallel with Banks's movements up the Valley turnpike, Schenck's objective being a junction with Milroy in an attack on Staunton. Fremont himself, with an additional force which he had collected at New River Depot (now called Keyser), on the Baltimore and Ohio Railroad, and at Romney, moved to Petersburg, 25 miles north of Franklin, through the mountains, establishing there a secondary base of supplies. All three columns had very limited wagon transportation and the roads were execrable.

These were the positions during the first week in May, 1862, when Jackson quietly slipped away from Elk Run Valley, leaving the ubiquitous Col. Turner Ashby's cavalry to entertain Banks's forces at Harrisonburg and New Market. Ewell's Division replaced Jackson's infantry near Conrad's Store and in Swift Run Gap, and remained there also to watch Banks at New Market and Harrisonburg.

Jackson moved up the east side of the Shenandoah to Brown's Gap, making very slow progress on account of the bad roads until he had passed through the Gap, but he conveyed the impression he had gone to reinforce Richmond. At Mechum's River Depot, near Charlottesville on the Virginia Central Railroad, he placed his troops on cars and rapidly conveyed them westward to Staunton, where, on the 5th of May, he effected a junction with Edward Johnson's Brigade, that had retired before Milroy from Monterey. The joint command was then 9,000 strong, and with it Jackson marched to McDowell, where he attacked Milroy on the 8th, Milroy being reinforced by about 1,500 men of Schenck's Brigade from Franklin shortly after the engagement opened, thus giving Milroy a force of about 3,500. Although outnumbered, Schenck and Milroy successfully resisted Jackson and Johnson throughout the day of the 8th, but retired slowly on Franklin, 30 miles, during the night and on the 9th, 10th and 11th, Jackson following and engaging them in their impregnable position at Franklin during the 12th and 13th, after which Jackson withdrew toward Staunton.

At McDowell the casualties were 498 Confederates (including 54 officers) and 256 Federals, the engagement lasting four hours, but Jackson claimed it as a victory because he held the field and saved Staunton. He also prevented a junction of Fremont's forces with Banks.

From Franklin, Jackson retraced his march through McDowell and came out of the mountains at Augusta Springs on the 15th of May, when, after resting his troops, he took the direct road to Harrisonburg via Mount Solon. He had taken the precaution to send parties along the eastern base of the Alleghenies northward to block the passes toward Moorefield, so that his flank would be secure against any attack that might come from the direction of Fremont's army at Franklin: On reaching the Valley Jackson ascertained that Banks's forces had all retired to Strasburg, leaving any movement he might make in that direction unopposed.

Jackson's departure from Elk Run Valley was only discovered by Banks through scouts, when, on the 5th of May, Banks fell back to New Market, under orders sent him by Mr. Stanton several days before, to retire his entire command to Strasburg, which latter place Banks reached on the 13th, leaving his cavalry at Woodstock, 12 miles south. Of Jackson's movement to Mechum's Depot[viii] and thence by rail to Staunton, his junction with Edward Johnson's command and his attack on Milroy at McDowell, Banks was entirely ignorant until he received, on the 12th, a dispatch from Fremont to Stanton, written at Petersburg, W. Va., the day before, telling of Schenck's position at Franklin, and Banks did not ascertain Jackson's whereabouts when the latter returned to the Valley until the 20th, when Fremont telegraphed him to that effect from Franklin, which information was corroborated the same day from New Market by Banks's own scouts.

At Strasburg, Banks had detached Shields's Division and sent it over the Manassas Gap Railroad to report to General McDowell. Geary's Brigade of Williams's Division, 1,500 strong, was guarding the railroad from Front Royal to Manassas, 52 miles, that line being visited occasionally by the enemy's cavalry from beyond the Rappahannock. Shields reached Manassas on the 18th of May, and marched from Catlett's, on the Orange and Alexandria Railroad, toward Fredericksburg on the 21st, reaching General McDowell at Fredericksburg on the 22d, where McDowell was concentrating a large force of 38,000 men to move on Richmond via Hanover Junction, in cooperation with McClellan's advance up the Peninsula. McDowell's only opponent would have been Gen. J. R. Anderson, with 11,000 men, at Massaponax.

Besides detaching Shields and Geary, Banks sent a regiment of Maryland infantry, 700 strong, two guns and a party of cavalry, under Colonel Kenly, to hold Front Royal, and posted one regiment on the railroad between Front Royal and Strasburg. This left Banks on the 21st of May with only about 7,000 men at Strasburg.

On the very day that Shields's Division reached Fredericksburg, May 22d, Jackson's and Ewell's commands, 18,000 strong, were marching on Front Royal via Luray, east of the Shenandoah River. Front Royal was attacked on the 23d and easily carried, the Maryland regiment holding it being cut up and driven out across the river toward Winchester, the enemy pursuing and capturing many prisoners. On the 24th, Jackson, with the main body, moved to Middletown from Cedarville, and placed his command on the turnpike five miles north of Strasburg and thirteen miles south of Winchester, expecting to interpose between Winchester and Banks at Strasburg, but the latter place was evacuated sufficiently early in the day to enable Banks to reach Winchester by 5 o'clock in the afternoon of the 24th, in advance of Jackson, saving the greater part of his trains, but losing some prisoners, being fiercely attacked while passing Middletown, Newtown and Kernstown.

Ewell, with part of the command, moved directly from Cedarville on Winchester. Both commands converging on Winchester were delayed by the resistance of Banks's retreating forces during the evening of the 24th and throughout the 25th until late in the day, when they entered Winchester, the Federals retiring toward Martinsburg, which they all reached during the afternoon, marching 22 miles; the enemy not pursuing with vigor.

Reaching the Potomac at Williamsport on the 26th, Banks[ix] safely crossed his trains and troops. His losses in killed, wounded and missing were 2,010. The enemy occupied Martinsburg with two regiments of cavalry, but his main force proceeded toward Harper's Ferry via Charlestown, reaching Halltown, three miles from Harper's Ferry, on the 28th, where he remained one day, but, beyond making a demonstration on Harper's Ferry, did not attack.

Then Jackson became uneasy, for both McDowell from the east and Fremont from the west, were marching to the relief of Banks, the former via Manassas and Front Royal, the latter from Franklin via Moorefield, while a large force—some 6,000 men—had been hastily assembled at Harper's Ferry under Gen. Rufus Saxton, to contest Jackson's further progress, and Banks was fast restoring his battered army at Williamsport.

The formation of McDowell's large force at Fredericksburg had caused General Lee, at Richmond, much uneasiness, for, with the exception of Ewell's command at Swift Run Gap, and Anderson's force near Fredericksburg, Northern Virginia had been depleted of Confederate troops. He sent two additional brigades to Gordonsville from Richmond (Branch and Mahone) early in May. McClellan had then reached the "White House," on the Pamunkey, and Lee desired at all hazards to prevent McDowell's advance to a junction with McClellan.

When Banks withdrew to Strasburg Lee believed it was for the purpose of abandoning the Valley and going to McDowell's army. Lee had already consulted Ewell and Jackson, before the latter went on his expedition against Milroy, concerning the expediency of a hurried joint movement towards Warrenton and Fredericksburg, especially in view of Banks's inertness, but Jackson held fast to his project of striking in detail first Milroy and then Banks.

The possibility of Banks leaving the Valley and joining McDowell or McClellan by way of Staunton was also considered, Jackson from Elk Run Valley, when reinforced by Ewell, intending, in case Banks pushed south from Harrisonburg, to move rapidly westward on New , Market, and not only place himself across Banks's route of supply but attack him in rear as well.

So, when Jackson had returned to the valley at Mount Solon, after having forced Milroy and Schenck back to Franklin, and he had learned of Banks's withdrawal to Strasburg, he hastily moved to the east side of the Shenandoah, and, taking Ewell with him, marched on Front Royal instead of directly on Strasburg, intending, no doubt, at least to prevent Banks from reaching McDowell across the Blue Ridge. Indeed, this scheme had been virtually communicated to Ewell by General Lee, during Jackson's absence, in a letter dated May 8th, and again to Jackson in a letter dated May 16th; furthermore, urging the breaking up of the Manassas Gap Railroad so as to prevent Banks's troops leaving the Valley by that route, but Shields had already passed through Front Royal eastward on the 16th.

A possible invasion of Maryland had been considered as feasible for Jackson in case Banks's army could have been overtaken and defeated. Accordingly, possibly to find and effect an unopposed crossing of the Potomac, Taylor's Brigade of Ewell's Division was detached by Jackson as he moved up towards Harper's Ferry, and sent into Loudoun County east of the Blue

Ridge. It was probably part of this force that attacked Geary's posts along the Manassas Gap Railroad.

Jackson also detached Ashby's Cavalry to proceed toward Moorefield, from which direction Fremont was reported to be coming; then, on the 31st of May, Jackson withdrew his main body from Halltown, marched rapidly through Winchester and Strasburg during the 1st of June, and thence up the Valley turnpike toward Harrisonburg, carrying with him 2,300 prisoners, 10,000 small arms and two pieces of artillery complete, captured principally from Banks's depots, Fremont's approach from near Wardensville being meanwhile effectually checked by Ewell's troops.

When Fremont joined Schenck and Milroy at Franklin, on the 13th of May, with Blenker's Division (then reduced to 6,000 men), Fremont's entire force numbered only 12,000. Blenker's Division, originally 10,000 strong, when detached from the Second Army Corps by McClellan, on the eve of his departure for the Peninsula, was composed mainly of Germans, and was sent to join Fremont by the President's direct order, evidently on account of some political pressure. To reach Fremont, Blenker had to march across country from Manassas to Harper's Ferry, thence to Winchester and Romney, mostly over bad roads, and with very defective transportation, camp equipage and clothing. So that when the division finally reached Fremont at Petersburg, W. Va., on the 9th day of May, it was in bad condition every way.

Fremont remained at Franklin until May 25th, getting his command in order, contemplating an expedition to break the Virginia and Tennessee Railroad somewhere between Salem and Newbern, then to turn toward Richmond. But on the 24th orders to move to Banks's assistance in the Shenandoah Valley were received, and Fremont moved in that direction via Moorefield and Wardensville, his advance reaching the later point on the 31st. He was then 15 miles west of Strasburg. Fremont was originally ordered to go to Harrisonburg from Franklin via Brock's Gap, but he came via Moorefield toward Strasburg instead.

On the 24th, also, McDowell at Fredericksburg was, very much to his disappointment, ordered to suspend his contemplated movement on Richmond via Hanover, and, instead, to detach 20,000 men to move westward to the succor of Banks via Front Royal, in which direction Shields started on the 25th to retrace his march; he reached Front Royal on the 30th, driving out the enemy and capturing 156 prisoners. Front Royal is 12 miles east of Strasburg. He sent his cavalry under Bayard toward Strasburg and moved his infantry up the Luray road to Conrad's Store, but Jackson had destroyed the bridges over the Shenandoah and the river was unfordable. Shields's advance was at Luray on the 6th of June.

Meanwhile, Fremont had moved into the valley near Strasburg, and on the 2d of June took up the pursuit of Jackson, who had eluded him, but whom he drove steadily before him through Woodstock, Edenburg and Mount Jackson, finally reaching Harrisonburg on the 6th. The enemy retreated to Port Republic, having abandoned much captured property and many prisoners during the pursuit, besides suffering many losses in killed and wounded during the many rear-guard actions, in one of which the gallant Ashby was among the killed, just beyond Harrisonburg, June 6th.

Fremont continued the march toward Port Republic on the 8th and became seriously engaged with the enemy at Cross Keys throughout the day, the losses on both sides being very large. The next day, the 9th, Fremont received delayed orders from Washington to halt at Harrisonburg.

Banks's army moving to the support of Fremont had made very slow progress from Williamsport. On the 8th of June it had only reached Winchester, where orders were sent Banks to move to Front Royal, sending troops to guard the Manassas Gap Railway eastward and to place an advance post at Luray.

On that date General Orders No. 62 of the War Department, series of 1862, was issued, changing the geographical limits of both Fremont's and Banks's commands as follows:

"The Mountain Department is extended eastward to the road running from Williamsport to Martinsburg, Winchester, Strasburg, Harrisonburg and Staunton, including that place; thence in the same direction southward until it reaches the Blue Ridge chain of mountains; thence with the line of the Blue Ridge to the southern boundary of the State of Virginia.

"The Department of the Shenandoah is extended eastward to include the Piedmont District and the Bull Run Mountain Range."

An additional division of troops, 6,000 strong, under Maj.-Gen. Franz Sigel,[x] reached Winchester via Harper's Ferry on the 4th of June, under orders to join Banks, but Sigel[xi] got to Winchester in advance of Banks, who was slowly marching there from Williamsport and Martinsburg.

Under his new orders Banks moved his main force to Front Royal, Shields's Division, as already noted, being at Luray and beyond. McDowell's troops, except Shields's, were then all withdrawn eastward.

While Fremont was engaging Jackson at Cross Keys, the head of Shields's Division was approaching Port Republic from the direction of Luray. His troops, in their effort to hasten the march, had become greatly attenuated and had lost cohesion. On the 9th the leading brigade, Tyler's, neared Port Republic, on the opposite side of the Shenandoah from Fremont. The enemy, after engaging Fremont, had moved from Cross Keys into Port Republic during the night and had destroyed the only bridge by which Fremont could cross and follow him.

Jackson then turned on Shields's approaching brigade and engaged it with such vigor that he forced it to retire upon the main body at Conrad's Store, after quite a spirited resistance and considerable loss, including seven guns.

Fremont established communication across the river with Shields's retreating troops and found they had received preparatory orders to return to Fredericksburg. The orders of the 9th to Fremont to withdraw to Harrisonburg and there act on the defensive, had only just reached him when he ascertained Shields's location and new orders. Considering the location of Harrisonburg imperfect for defensive purposes, and being seriously crippled by his losses at Cross Keys, besides hearing nothing from Banks, Fremont decided to retire to Mount Jackson where he arrived on the 12th of June, his action receiving the President's approval.

Subsequently, on the 24th of June, Banks withdrew to Middletown, and on the 27th he asked to be relieved from service under Major General Pope, who, by orders of the President, dated June 26th, had been called from the West and placed in command of all the troops covering Washington, including those in the Shenandoah Valley.

During this campaign, from May 23 to June 9, 1862, Jackson's troops had over 1,500 casualties. Fremont's losses were 684, Banks's 2,019 and Shields's 1,018.

As Fremont withdrew from Port Republic Jackson followed him closely with his cavalry, now commanded by Munford, making always a show of strength and never losing contact. Jackson's infantry, which had certainly been overworked both by marching and by fighting, was concentrated at and near Mount Meridian, where they were enabled to get a few days of rest before being moved again, this .time, by Lee's orders, toward Richmond and the Pamunkey River, whither, whilst great secrecy covered the movement, they were rapidly transferred by rail and by marching, and arrived at Ashland, near their destination, on the 25th of June.

Fremont (12,000) was then at Middletown, Banks (12,500) at and near Front Royal, McDowell was gathering a new army at Fredericksburg and McClellan was on the Chickahominy. The only Confederate troops left in the Valley were some of Munford's cavalry, which, later, were also withdrawn.

Jackson's correspondence with General Lee and his instructions to his Chief of Cavalry, Munford, reveal how great was the desire of the Richmond authorities that Jackson should retire from the Shenandoah as secretly and as rapidly as possible, to reinforce the Confederate Army confronting McClellan before Richmond. The Union records show how successful Jackson and his subordinates were in impressing Fremont, Banks and Stanton that another invasion of the lower Valley was impending, long after Jackson had taken off all his infantry and artillery toward

Richmond, including Lawton's and Whiting's Brigades, which had recently come to Jackson as reinforcements from Lee's army. With his own and Ewell's Divisions, strengthened by Lawton's and Whiting's Brigades (14 regiments of about 8,500 men), Jackson carried to Lee an army of over 25,000. He left his cavalry, under Munford and about 5,000 strong, supported by some few infantry and dismounted men, to demonstrate down the Valley and at New Market or Luray, toward Fremont's and Shields's retiring columns at Strasburg and Front Royal. Munford allowed only those to pass his lines northward who were sent purposely to take false information of the most exaggerated character, to cover and conceal the movement of Jackson toward Lee. How little true information the Federal troops received during the ten days following Jackson's departure is shown by the dispatches sent to and from Washington by Stanton, Fremont and Banks.

By the 20th of June Fremont had his army of 12,000 men at and west of Strasburg, while Banks at Middletown had his two divisions (Sigel and Williams) about 13,000 strong extended along the north bank of the Shenandoah and Cedar Creek, from Front Royal to Middletown. (Later, all this force except one small brigade kept at Winchester, another brigade at Martinsburg and still another at Harper's Ferry, was sent east of the Blue Ridge to Pope, who had been assigned, June 26th, by the President to a new command, designated the Army of Virginia, and embracing the troops in the Valley, of Fremont and Banks, together with those of McDowell, between the Blue Ridge and Fredericksburg. Fremont was relieved, at his own request, from the subordinate command contemplated by the President's order, and left the army in the field. Banks and McDowell loyally accepted their new assignments as corps commanders under Pope, although they, as well as Fremont, had previously been commanding separate departments, now abolished.

The Confederates relieved Munford's cavalry with Robertson's, at Harrisonburg and New Market, so as to enable the former to rejoin Jackson.

The Valley then enjoyed comparative quiet throughout July and August of 1862, but in September, with Lee's advance to the Rapidan and Pope's subsequent defeat at Bull Run, came a renewal of the disturbed conditions for which the Shenandoah had become famous.

TABLE OF DISTANCES
Miles.

Mount Jackson to Strasburg 22
Strasburg to Winchester 18
Winchester to Harper's Ferry 28
Strasburg to Elk Run Valley 50
Elk Run Valley to Mechum's Station 60
Staunton to Bull Pasture Mountain (McDowell) 32
Bull Pasture Mountain to Franklin 30
Bull Pasture Mountain to Augusta

Springs 10
Augusta Springs to New Market 42
New Market to Luray 12
Luray to Front Royal 29
Front Royal to Harper's Ferry 57
Strasburg to Woodstock 12
Woodstock to Mount Jackson 12
Mount Jackson to New Market 7
New Market to Port Republic 30
Port Republic to Brown's Gap 12
Brown's Gap to Mount Meridian 10
Mount Meridian to Ashland 120

Looking backward, after forty years, at this wonderful Valley campaign of 1862, the military student cannot fail to be impressed with the audacity and strategical eminence of Stonewall Jackson, as compared with the lack of capacity and want of cohesion on the part of his opponents.

On the Federal side the day had not yet dawned for the military leaders to disappear who had been sent to command armies in the. field through political or social influence. Latent military talent had not yet sufficiently developed itself among those having neither political nor social influence to justify the authorities at Washington to call it to the chief commands, and, unfortunately, those same authorities had not yet recovered from the shock and surprises of the year before; they were still groping for suitable commanders for the thousands of ardent but inexperienced soldiers who only asked to be led against the enemy.

For a past-master in the art of war like Jackson to handle an army, no matter how inferior in strength, against generals of the military calibre of Patterson, Banks, Fremont, or Pope, was not difficult, for he was of the Cromwellian type, who fought as sincerely as he prayed, and looked for no ulterior reward; whereas those leaders against whom he operated had been selected either to gratify a political faction or to please a military clique, and who hoped to secure either professional advancement or political preferment.

Taking into consideration Jackson's situation May 29th and 30th, with his army of 16,000 men thundering away at Halltown for possession of Harper's Ferry, only three miles distant, and threatening to cross into Maryland or attack Washington through the passes of the Blue Ridge; with Banks's shattered army of 7,000 men reorganizing at Williamsport, but. threatening Jackson on his left flank and front; Saxton, with a hastily gathered but incongruous force of 6,000 men, sturdily barring Jackson's progress at Harper's Ferry; McDowell, with 20,000 men, on his right rear, approaching Front Royal from Manassas; while Fremont, with 12,000 men, was debouching into the Valley from Wardensville on his left rear, —a weakhearted, incompetent commander would then have made a precipitate retreat toward his base, with consequent demoralization and disaster.

Not so Jackson, for when he found his position no longer tenable in front of Harper's Ferry he rapidly, but no less cohesively, retraced his march through

Winchester and Strasburg to Mount Jackson and Harrisonburg, taking with him safely an immense wagon train of munitions of war and 2,300 prisoners, captured from the enemy.

With all this impedimenta he was passing Strasburg on the 1st of June, when Fremont was only ten miles away toward Wardensville on his right and McDowell was at Front Royal only twelve miles away on his left, but the Valley was clear ahead of him and Banks made no effort to fall upon his rear. A more desperate situation, so successfully solved, would be difficult to find in the annals of war.

CHAPTER V

The Capitulation of Harper's Ferry

Pope's army had been defeated at Bull Run during the last days of August, 1862, and had sought shelter within the defenses of Washington, where it was reorganized by McClellan and made ready to take the field again, this time north of the Potomac.

After dispersing Pope's command, and realizing the futility of either attacking the fortifications of Washington or of besieging that city, Lee determined upon an invasion of Maryland and possibly of Pennsylvania.

In his letters to President Davis of September 3 and 4, 1862, Lee states his opinion that the time was then propitious for such a movement, "to give material aid to Maryland and afford her an opportunity of throwing off the oppression to which she is now subject." On the 3d of September this project was commenced by Lee moving his elated army to Leesburg, where, from the 4th to the 7th, his troops crossed the Potomac at the fords and ferries of that vicinity and headed for Frederick, without demonstrating toward either Washington or Baltimore.

As early as September 2, before Lee's northern march had commenced, General Halleck ordered the troops occupying Winchester to retire down the Valley to Harper's Ferry and prepare to hold that position as well as Martinsburg, at least temporarily. But this arrangement was contrary to the expectation of General Lee, who had believed that his movement into Maryland would force the entire evacuation of the Shenandoah and give him an unobstructed route of communication through the Valley to Richmond. To remove this obstruction became imperative.

McClellan, meanwhile, became aware of Lee's movement into Maryland and prepared to cover Washington and Baltimore from attack north of the Potomac by interposing his army between those cities and Lee's forces, until Lee's ultimate intentions could be disclosed. A large force was left to defend Washington, in case Lee's Maryland movement should prove only a feint to attack, with another force, the Capital itself. These precautions rendered the advance of McClellan toward Lee very slow, as he moved his army westward toward Frederick, between the Potomac and the Baltimore and Ohio Railroad, so that it was only late on the 12th that McClellan's advanced troops entered Frederick, unopposed, Lee having moved two days before through Hagerstown, westward into the passes of South Mountain (a continuation of the Blue Ridge north of the Potomac).

All this while the position at Harper's Ferry gave the authorities at Washington great uneasiness, especially when it became known to them that Lee, at Frederick, on the 10th or September, had detached a very large force under Jackson (Stonewall) to re-cross the Potomac at Williamsport, to operate against Harper's Ferry and clear a route for Lee's possible return to Virginia.

McClellan, on the 11th, at Rockville, when it was already too late, asked Halleck to order the garrison of Harper's Ferry to join him, but this Halleck declined to do, although the next day (the 12th) Halleck transferred that garrison from Wool's Department to McClellan's, to take effect as soon as he (McClellan) "could open communication" with the place.

The Federal commander of Harper's Ferry (Col. Dixon S. Miles), with a garrison of 10,000 men, had strict instructions from Wool to hold the place at all hazards, at least until he could be succored from McClellan's advancing army. Maryland Heights, overlooking Harper's Ferry, had been partly fortified and was occupied by a small detachment of Miles's troops, the remainder of his forces being entrenched on Bolivar Heights and in the town of Harper's Ferry.

No one could be more familiar with the possibilities of defending Harper's Ferry, or of its untenableness, than was Jackson, for he had been sent there early in 1861, and, after fully studying the situation, had advised against its retention except by an exceedingly strong force. It is therefore presumable that when Lee selected him to reduce the position, he (Jackson) insisted on being provided with a heavy body of troops. So Lee sent from Frederick one-half of his army, six divisions (A. P. Hill's, Ewell's and Starke's), to move via Williamsport and Martinsburg, while McLaws's

Division, supported by Anderson's, occupied Maryland Heights from the north, and Walker's Division was ordered by way of Cheek's Ford of the Potomac to occupy Loudoun Heights. Walker was prevented "by the enemy" from crossing at Cheek's, so he crossed at Point of Rocks during the night of the 10th instead, and got into position on Loudoun Heights, which he found unoccupied, during the night of the 13th, effectually barring any escape of the garrison of Harper's Ferry down the south side of the Potomac.

McLaws, with his own and Anderson's Division, moved on the 10th (via Crampton's Gap of South Mountain and Pleasant Valley, Maryland) to take position on Maryland Heights and the debouche of the Valley along the Potomac at Sandy Hook and Weverton. He forced the retreat into Harper's Ferry of the troops on Maryland Heights, after some resistance, on the 13th, and succeeded in getting some guns into position there, after considerable labor, that effectually commanded Harper's Ferry. His troops in Pleasant Valley moved forward to the Potomac and thus closed all egress north or east to Miles's forces, north of the Potomac.

On the 14th Franklin's Corps of McClellan's army reached and forced the passage of Crampton's Gap, only seven miles north of Maryland Heights, and advanced a short distance down Pleasant Valley toward Harper's Ferry, when Franklin most unaccountably halted, went into camp and did not attack McLaws on the 15th, although McLaws had drawn up six small brigades across the Valley near Crampton's Gap and invited attack. McLaws also had four brigades at Weverton and Sandy Hook, besides the force on top of Maryland Heights, which latter was firing down into Harper's Ferry.

This Federal force in Pleasant Valley on the 14th and 15th consisted of Franklin's (Sixth) Army Corps and Crouch's Division (three large divisions of three brigades each), and was 20,000 strong. It did not even follow up McLaws' weaker force when, on the 15th, the latter crossed his troops and trains into Harper's Ferry after the capitulation.

The main movement to reduce Harper's Ferry was conducted by Jackson in person, and consisted, as already mentioned, of three divisions, which, after crossing the Potomac at Williamsport on the 11th, moved on Martinsburg and down the south side of the river. The Federal garrison of Martinsburg, under Gen. Julius White, evacuated the place during the night of the 11th, safely reached Harper's Ferry on the 12th, closely followed by Jackson's troops, however, who reached Halltown, three miles south of Harper's Ferry, on the 13th, where Miles's forces were found drawn up on Bolivar Heights nearby.

The withdrawal of the garrisons of Winchester and Martinsburg gave Miles at Harper's Ferry a force of nearly 13,000 men. The six divisions of the enemy, surrounding him on all sides, could not have numbered less than 30,000, for they were all composed of more than three brigades each, some having five or six.

On joining Miles, for some magnanimous reason which Miles seems to have greatly appreciated, General White presented the most unusual example of not claiming command of all the Federal troops at Harper's Ferry, by virtue of his superior rank, but generously waived it, instead, on the ground that Miles was more thoroughly familiar with the situation and had already made all preparations to defend the place. White then most loyally assumed command of only part of the line and gave Miles conscientious support to the end.

That end came on the morning of the 15th, when the Confederate lines had been more closely drawn around the position, which was also enfiladed from several directions by the enemy's artillery. At Miles's request, after taking a unanimous vote of his council of war, White negotiated with Jackson the terms of capitulation, which surrendered over 11,000 men as prisoners of war, besides a vast quantity of arms and stores. It was after the white flags of surrender had actually gone up that Miles was mortally wounded by a shell fired from one of the Confederate batteries and the command then devolved on White.

Lee, in his report, says that "the advance of the Federal army was so slow at the time we left Fredericktown [September 10] as to justify the belief that the reduction of Harper's Ferry could be accomplished and our troops concentrated before they would be called upon to meet it." Lee retained with him only Longstreet's, D. H. Hill's and his cavalry corps, after detaching Jackson's three divisions, as well as McLaws's, Anderson's and Walker's. On the 13th and 14th Lee was attacked by McClellan's advance at the Gap in South Mountain on the Boonesborough pike, during the absence of his six divisions operating against Harper's Ferry, but as McClellan did not push his attack with sufficient vigor, Lee succeeded in checking McClellan as well as preventing any relief going to Harper's Ferry. He became uneasy, however, and dispatched couriers to hasten the return of all his detachments, Jackson rejoining him at Sharpsburg on the 16th, where Lee had retreated on the 15th. Jackson left A. P. Hill's Division temporarily at Harper's Ferry, but Hill's, as well as McLaws's, Anderson's and Walker's Divisions, returned to Lee's main army at Sharpsburg on the 16th and 17th.

McClellan's army came up to the Antietam during the afternoon of the 15th, but made no attack on Lee beyond some artillery firing until late on the 16th, after Jackson and Walker had rejoined Longstreet and D. H. Hill at Sharpsburg. The Battle of Antietam came off on the 17th.

Lee says, "The resistance that had been offered to the enemy at Boonesborough Gap secured sufficient time to enable General Jackson to complete the reduction of Harper's Ferry." The engagement at Boonesborough is known to us officially as the Battle of South

Mountain. It certainly enabled Lee to reunite his troops and meet McClellan behind the Antietam.

During the night of the 18th Lee's army re-crossed the Potomac into Virginia, near Shepherdstown; he was covered by his cavalry under J. E. B. Stuart. An effort of Porter's Federal Corps to cross and pursue was repulsed by A. P. Hill's Division on the 20th. Lee then moved his army slowly to Martinsburg, Bunker Hill and Winchester, the Federals reoccupying the line of the Potomac and Harper's Ferry, "but made no other forward movement. It was during this period of inactivity, in the early days of October, that Stuart crossed the Potomac above Williamsport with his cavalry, about 1,500 strong, and made his successful raid on Chambersburg, re-crossing again into Virginia below Harper's Ferry, without loss or interference by the Federal cavalry. Stuart passed entirely around McClellan's army, just as he had done earlier in the summer on the Peninsula.

No amount of urging, ordering or pleading by Lincoln could induce McClellan to move south of the upper Potomac until the last days of October, when he crossed his army at Berlin, below Harper's Ferry, and moved south along the eastern base of the Blue Ridge, occupying some of the gaps as far south as Snicker's, to protect his flanks, but not to threaten Lee, whose army still remained near Winchester. McClellan's objective point was still Richmond, but as he moved with characteristic ponderousness and elaboration, Lee immediately sent Longstreet's Corps (half his army) by Front Royal through Chester Gap to Culpeper Court House, to which point he transferred his own headquarters on the 6th of November, leaving Jackson (with the other half of his army) in the Valley to threaten either another invasion of Maryland or McClellan's flank and his communications with Washington, should the latter advance far enough southward.

McClellan left Slocum's Corps to hold Harper's Ferry and placed three additional brigades at Sharpsburg, Williamsport and above. These troops were intended mainly to observe and guard the crossings of the Potomac, but they also made an occasional reconnaissance toward the enemy at Berryville, Winchester or Martinsburg.

From Snicker's Gap McClellan deflected his army to the line of the Manassas Gap Railroad and fixed his own headquarters first at Rectortown. His base was then at Alexandria, whence his supplies came by rail. On the 9th of November General McClellan was superseded in command of the Army of the Potomac, at Warrenton, by General Burnside.

Lee still retained Jackson in the Valley about Berryville and Winchester, but prepared to rapidly move through the upper passes of the Blue Ridge to unite with Longstreet at Culpeper, should Burnside attempt to interpose between them by moving on Culpeper in force, or, in case Burnside moved on Fredericksburg, down the Rappahannock, Jackson was to rejoin Lee by the shortest practicable route. Jackson drew his supplies from Staunton and Lee from Richmond.

On the 19th of November and again on the 23d, Lee wrote to Jackson that he considered it advisable for him to leave the Valley and bring his corps of 35,000 men east of the Blue Ridge to a point nearer Fredericksburg, where Lee had gone in person, and from which point it was expected Burnside's assembled army would try to force its way to Richmond.

Jackson left a small force, principally Marylanders under Steuart, and some cavalry, to hold Winchester and the lower Valley, and then moved up the Valley through Strasburg and New Market to Swift Run Gap, where he crossed the Blue Ridge and reported his troops to Lee from Orange Court-House on the 27th of November. The next day General Lee directed Jackson to move his command to a position near the railroad from Fredericksburg to Richmond, on Massaponax Creek, as at that time Lee did not believe Burnside would endeavor to cross the Rappahannock at Fredericksburg, but would select a crossing at some point below—possibly Port Royal.

A strong reconnaissance, sent out December 1 from Harper's Ferry, under Geary, went through Charlestown to Berryville and thence to Winchester, returning to Harper's Ferry via Bunker Hill and Smithfield. Geary encountered some resistance along his route from the Seventh and Twelfth Virginia Cavalry, the infantry troops (about 2,000 Marylanders) evacuating Winchester and moving south toward Strasburg when Geary entered Winchester on the 4th of December. Geary soon withdrew and the Confederates reoccupied the town.

A small reconnaissance made from New Creek to Moorefield, on the same dates as the above, found two companies of partisan cavalry under McDonald, which were dispersed, after killing two, wounding several and capturing ten.

Another small cavalry reconnaissance through Martinsburg, toward Darkesville, on the 11th of December, captured thirteen prisoners and dispersed three companies of the Seventh Confederate Cavalry to Bunker Hill.

On the 9th of December General Burnside ordered Slocum to withdraw his troops from Harper's Ferry and march via Leesburg to Centerville where he was to report to General Sigel as part of the reserve of Burnside's army. Morell, who, from his headquarters at Hagerstown, commanded the defenses of the upper Potomac, was directed to replace Slocum's troops at Harper's Ferry with Kenly's[xii] brigade of Marylanders, and at the same time another force was to reoccupy Martinsburg. On the 16th of December Morell was relieved by Gen. B. F. Kelley, whose command at Cumberland was extended to include all the line of the Baltimore and Ohio Railroad from New Creek (now Keyser) to Harper's Ferry. The railroad was then being rebuilt into Martinsburg from the west.

Kelley fixed his headquarters mostly at Harper's Ferry. He had, besides his own brigade and local garrisons between Cumberland and Grafton and Kenly's Maryland Brigade at Harper's Ferry, a force of eight regiments under Milroy, recently arrived at New Creek from the region between Monterey and Beverly, west of the Alleghenies. Milroy was sent to reinforce the troops on the railroad east of Cumberland when Jackson was still about Winchester, and who threatened further interruption of the railroad west of Martinsburg as well as to carry out Jackson's favorite hobby of an invasion of the territory in West Virginia containing his original home, at Clarksburg.

From New Creek Kelley sent, December 6, one brigade from this column of Milroy's to reoccupy Petersburg, W. Va., southeast from the Baltimore and Ohio Railroad toward Franklin and Monterey, and later sent the remainder of Milroy's command in the same general direction, so that by the end of December Milroy's forces occupied Romney, Moorefield, Petersburg and up the valley of the south fork of the Potomac, while with his mounted troops under Cluseret (later celebrated as one of the leaders of the Commune in France), he took possession of Winchester. Kelley also repaired and reopened the Baltimore and Ohio Railroad eastward from Hancock to Harper's Ferry.

The inaction of the Army of the Potomac under Burnside, after his unsuccessful assault at Fredericksburg, might have enabled Lee to dispatch troops for service elsewhere. Notwithstanding the severity of the winter and the dreadful condition of the roads, some enterprising cavalry raids were made by Lee's troops to the rear of Burnside's army, one small party under Rosser penetrating into the Shenandoah almost to Martinsburg, but returning east of the Blue Ridge immediately.

The Confederate forces in the Shenandoah consisted mainly of cavalry, supported by some Maryland infantry, all under command of Gen. W. E. Jones, and numbering about 2,500 in all. This force had retired to New Market late in December of 1862, but early in January, by General Lee's orders, made an unsuccessful attempt to drive back the Federal forces at Moorefield and Petersburg, having McNeill's Company of Imboden's partisan cavalry from the direction of Monterey, to cooperate with him.

Realizing the difficulty of maintaining too many detached positions, General Kelley removed the troops from Petersburg and Moorefield to strengthen those at Romney, soon after Jones was beaten off, recognizing the importance of Romney and Winchester as outposts for the protection of the newly-reconstructed Baltimore and Ohio Railroad from the west through Martinsburg. Again, Romney was only 26 miles east from New Creek, whence the command drew its supplies, and was as important an outpost for New Creek and Cumberland as it was for Winchester. From Romney cavalry could penetrate southward, up the fertile valley of the south fork of the Potomac, as far as

Monterey, and thence to the Virginia Central Railroad.

On the 19th of January, 1863, all movements south of the Winchester line were ordered stopped, as the Washington authorities did not desire any cause to be given Lee to detach any portion of his army then confronting Burnside.

The reoccupation of the lower Valley by the Union forces and the reopening of the Baltimore and Ohio Railroad gave General Lee great concern, so he endeavored, as the winter closed in, to detach to the support of his troops about New Market, up the Valley, such of the Confederate forces at Staunton and the Lewisburg or Huttonsville lines as could be spared. Burnside's rapidly increasing army in his front, though inactive, perplexed Lee.

On the 25th of January, 1863, orders were issued, by direction of the President, superseding General Burnside in command of the Army of the Potomac by Gen. Joseph Hooker.

CHAPTER VI
Jones's and Imboden's Raid into West Virginia

Both armies remained inactive at Fredericksburg, after Hooker assumed command of the Federal army, until the latter part of April, 1863, when Hooker attempted to turn Lee's left flank and was badly defeated at Chancellorsville.

Meanwhile, the small force of Confederates in the Valley, under Col. W. E. Jones, was as active as the severe weather and their weak strength permitted, while Milroy had his headquarters and main force at Winchester, with outposts at Berryville, Strasburg, and Romney, throughout the winter of 1862-'63.

Jones had his headquarters first at New Market and then at Lacey Springs, near Harrisonburg, from either place being within communication with J. E. B. Stuart's cavalry headquarters at Culpeper, on the Orange and Alexandria Railroad.

During the winter General Lee organized an expedition, to be sent from the Valley as soon as the spring opened, to destroy the Baltimore and Ohio Railroad west of Cumberland. It had been General Lee's unremitting endeavor from the beginning of hostilities to interrupt Federal communication with the West by that railroad, especially at the Cheat River viaduct at Rowlesburg.

The expedition for 1863 was to consist of two cooperating columns, one under W. E. Jones to move via Brock's Gap and Lost River down the South Fork of the Potomac through Moorefield, and thence toward Cheat River Viaduct; the other, under a noted "partisan ranger," Imboden, to be formed near Monterey and Hightown, on the Parkersburg turnpike, to move over the mountains northwest through Beverly in the same general direction as the Jones column, which was to move on the Northwestern turnpike.

In the correspondence of General Lee of this period it appears he was becoming very much impressed with the feats of a noted guerilla (or partisan) named J. H. McNeill, who operated in the region about Moorefield and Romney. McNeill was one of Imboden's captains and had made several daring and successful forays.

To get an understanding of the status of the Confederate "partisan rangers," as distinguished from the regular soldier, consultation of Confederate legislation and the correspondence arising therefrom, is necessary. There was nothing similar in the United States service.

We find first that Virginia as early as March 27, 1862, by an act of the General Assembly, authorized the forming "of ten or more companies of rangers," of 100 men each, "to be composed exclusively of men whose homes are in the districts overrun by the public enemy, within the limits of said counties, who shall enlist for twelve months in the service of this Commonwealth, to act as rangers and scouts on our exposed frontier near the lines of the enemy. The said officers and privates shall receive the same pay as is allowed to the privates and officers by the Confederate States. shall be under the command of the Governor, and shall conform their operations to the usages of civilized warfare. Whenever the said rangers shall be in the neighborhood of a Confederate army, they shall be subject to the orders of the commandant of the same and shall always cooperate with the movements of said army when ordered to do so."

Within a month, April 21, 1862, the Confederate Congress passed an act "to organize bands of partisan rangers throughout the Confederacy, in companies, battalions, or regiments, either as infantry or cavalry," and to "be entitled to the same pay, rations and quarters as other soldiers. That for any arms and munitions of war captured from the enemy by anybody of partisan rangers and delivered to any quartermaster the rangers shall be paid their full value."

It will be observed, by the last clause of the foregoing act, the rangers received a premium for capturing property not allowed "other soldiers." Also that they were not required to confine their operations to any particular region of the country, but might enter the enemy's territory at will.

Then, too, the Confederate Congress was silent about the ranger conforming his operations "to the usages of civilized warfare." The "public defense" acts absorbed into the Confederate army all troops that had been raised under State authority, including the rangers, although these latter were never brigaded with other troops, but operated, under their own officers, independently.

These independent commands, with their freedom from all the restraints and discipline of the line, soon made the partisan service very popular to serve in, so much so that the Confederate War Department found it necessary to restrict the partisan service to persons not liable to conscription and to forbid any transfer from other branches of the army. Also to endeavor to exclude from the partisan .corps • deserters from the regulars, of whom there were already great numbers in hiding throughout the Confederacy as early as 1862.

The Virginia Assembly, on the 28th of February, 1863, transferred all State troops and rangers to the Confederate Government and stopped their further enlistments under State authority.

There were ninety-five companies of rangers registered at the Confederate War Department on the 12th of September, 1863, with many more in process of formation.

The operation of the Ranger Act was not long in making itself felt to the detriment of the Confederate Army, as shown by the reports and correspondence of both army and civilian officials, but all attacks upon the system proved unavailing until the acts organizing these guerilla forces were revoked by the Confederate Congress, February 17, 1864, exception being then made to retain such as were acting as regular cavalry. Of these, McNeill's Company and Mosby's Battalion were continued in service as partisans.

It is presumed the action taken by the Confederate Congress was finally reached through consideration of the annual report of the Secretary of War, James A. Seddon, dated Richmond, November 26, 1863, where he mentions the rangers as follows:

"The advantages anticipated from the allowance of corps of partisan rangers, with peculiar privileges of prize to stimulate their zeal and activity, have been very partially realized, while from their independent organization and the facilities and temptations thereby afforded to license and depredations, grave mischiefs have resulted. They have, indeed, when under inefficient officers and operating within our own limits, come to be regarded as more formidable and destructive to our own people than to the enemy. The opportunities, too, afforded them of profit by their captures, as well as the lighter bonds of discipline under which they are held, serve to dissatisfy the trained soldiers of the Provisional Army, who, encountering greater perils and privations, are denied similar indulgences. There are certainly some honorable exceptions to the general estimate thus held of the partisan corps, and in several instances partisan leaders have distinguished themselves and their corps by services as eminent as their achievements have been daring and brilliant. They constitute only notable exceptions, and experience of the general inefficiency and even mischief of the organizations would recommend that they either be merged in the troops of the line or be disbanded and conscripted. To preserve the few that are valuable coadjutors to the general service, discretion may be entrusted to the Department."

General Lee was very much of the same opinion, for April 1, 1864, he writes to Adjutant-General Cooper, recommending that all rangers, except Mosby's Battalion, be disbanded, and saying:

"Experience has convinced me that it is almost impossible, under the best officers even, to have discipline in these bands of partisan rangers, or to prevent them from becoming an injury instead of a benefit to the service, and even where this is accomplished, the system gives license to many deserters and marauders, who assume to belong to these authorized companies, and commit depredations on friend and foe alike. Another great objection to them is the bad effect upon the discipline of the army, from the constant desire of the men to leave their regiments and enjoy the great license allowed in these bands."

It was to one of these partisan leaders, however, that General Lee entrusted in April, 1863, the main column for the raid on the Baltimore and Ohio Railroad, as we find in his correspondence with Col. J. D. Imboden, Capt. J. H. McNeill (both partisans), and with the two Joneses (both regulars).

Imboden, at Staunton, had in June, 1862, raised four full companies of the ranger regiment he had been authorized to recruit, and was told by the Secretary of War to organize the men he already had into a battalion and afterwards increase it to a regiment. He was getting his recruits mainly from the mountain districts east and west of the Alleghenies.

On the 3d of February, 1863, General Lee addressed a letter to Imboden, as "General Commanding Northwest Brigade," congratulating him on his promotion and urging him "to bring out all the men subject to military duty in the Northwest. I think it unnecessary to caution you against receiving men who have deserted from other companies or regiments." Referring to the enemy, General Lee continues: "He cannot during the winter move with any large infantry force across the mountains against you. I am very anxious to drive him out of the Valley, and desire you to be prepared to cooperate with Gen. W. E. Jones whenever an opportunity occurs."

On the 2d of March, Imboden, from his camps near McDowell and Monterey, submitted to General Lee a plan of an expedition to destroy all the bridges of the Baltimore and Ohio Railroad between Oakland and Grafton, and then to move against the enemy at Beverly, Philippi, and Buckhannon, in West Virginia, the enemy at that period not being in strong force at any point on that line. Imboden proposed to start with 2,500 men and extra arms for 1,500 additional, whom he expected would join him as soon as he reached Beverly and beyond. For the latter purpose, Imboden asked that the Twenty-fifth and Thirty-first Virginia Infantry, composed mainly of refugees from that section of country, be sent to him for the movement, and whose ranks, as well as those of his own rangers, Imboden hoped to fill up while in West Virginia.

As a collateral movement, Gen. W. E. Jones, commanding the Valley District, was to press the enemy down the Shenandoah toward Winchester and then move rapidly on Romney, New Creek (Keyser), and Cumberland. While Jones was doing this Imboden was to send a mounted flying column of 500 men, probably under the celebrated J. H. McNeill, to move through Moorefield to Oakland on the railroad by the Northwest turnpike, but avoiding the enemy at New Creek. Meanwhile, Imboden, with his infantry and artillery, would move from Monterey on Huttonsville and Beverly, west of the mountains, while his cavalry with McNeill was cutting and destroying the Cheat River Viaduct and the trestle work on the railroad. The enemy at Beverly was to be forced out toward Weston or Clarksburg, so as to enable the party operating on the railroad to rejoin the dismounted men south of Grafton.

If successful, Imboden expected to be joined by thousands of recruits and to collect for the Confederate Army large numbers of horses and cattle.

This plan was promptly approved by General Lee and preparations for its execution commenced as early as March n, but the severe winter and the condition of the mountain roads and streams delayed the departure of either Imboden or Jones until the last week in April, and then with the original plan somewhat modified. Gen. Sam Jones, commanding the Department of West Virginia, was ordered to supply some troops to Imboden and otherwise assist him by threatening the enemy's positions on the Kanawha, and preventing reinforcements going from that point to the Baltimore and Ohio Railroad.

So much did General Lee have in mind the regaining of the lower Valley that, while writing confidentially from Fredericksburg to President Davis of army matters generally, he says, on the 2d of April, "when the roads permit of our moving, unless in the meantime General Hooker takes the aggressive, I propose to make a blow at Milroy, which, I think, will draw General Hooker out, or at least prevent further reinforcements being sent to the West." At that time Burnside had taken 20,000 men of the Ninth Army Corps from the east to Cincinnati by rail, where he was organizing an expedition to march on Knoxville, in cooperation with a forward movement from Murfreesborough, in Middle Tennessee, by Rosecrans's army.

At that same time General Lee was having great trouble in subsisting his army, so that he urged upon all the detached commanders in the field, especially "the partisans," to collect horses, cattle, provisions, etc., from the country in which they operated. As "munitions of war" had been construed by the Confederate authorities to include everything needed by an army, an additional incentive for indiscriminate plundering was held out to the partisans, for, by the law creating them, they received prize money for all stores captured by them and turned in to proper authority.

Imboden finally got started on the 20th of April, 1863, from Shenandoah Mountain and Monterey, over the main range of the Allegheny Mountains toward Beverly. He had a mixed command of nearly 3,500 men, regulars and partisans (of which latter 700 were mounted) and he had six guns. About half this force had been furnished by Gen. Sam Jones.

W. E. Jones moved from Lacey Springs, in the Upper Shenandoah Valley, on the 21st of April, by way of Brock's Gap and Lost River, toward Moorefield. The plan submitted by Imboden had been modified, so that, instead of pressing the enemy toward Winchester and then passing through Romney, Jones was to avoid both those places, as well as New Creek, and move rapidly for the railroad at Oakland. Jones says he took "all my [his] available strength in cavalry, infantry and artillery," but fails to mention his actual strength, which was probably not less than 3,500 men. Of these, he sent back about 1,000 from Moorefield, when he could not get all his command over the Potomac on account of high water. Before starting, all men and horses unfit for a hard campaign were left behind in the Valley, under Lieut.-Col. O. R. Funsten,

Eleventh Virginia Cavalry, who had his outposts extended well toward Strasburg, and where, on the 28th of April, he had a brisk skirmish with some of Milroy's troops.

Jones reached Moorefield on the 24th of April, the same day that Imboden, on the other side of the mountains, was attacking Beverly. Jones found no enemy at Moorefield but the river was too high to cross, so he was forced to make a detour of eleven miles upstream to Petersburg, where he succeeded in getting most of his mounted men over after considerable difficulty. The dismounted men, artillery and trains, as well as some three hundred of his cavalry, not being able to cross at all, were sent back to the Shenandoah Valley by way of Franklin, gathering up all surplus bacon, etc., along the route. With the bulk of his mounted force, consisting of the First Maryland and White's Virginia Battalions, the Sixth, Seventh and Twelfth Virginia, and some of McNeill's partisans, in all about 2,500 men, Jones resumed his movement on Oakland.

He was obliged to pass through Greenland Gap, in the Knobley Mountain, 20 miles west of Moorefield, to get onto the Northwestern turnpike and to avoid the strong force of Federal troops at New Creek (Keyser). Most unexpectedly, Jones found at the Gap a small and stubborn detachment of eighty-three Infantry, under Capt. Martin Wallace of the Twenty-third Illinois (Irish Brigade), who, from a church and a log house in the Gap, delayed Jones half a day on the 25th and only yielded when the buildings were set on fire by Jones's men, after darkness enabled them to crawl up close enough. Three previous assaults had been repulsed with considerable loss to the Confederates, including Col. R. H. Dulaney, Seventh Virginia Cavalry, wounded, and several of his officers. Wallace says the Confederates lost 104 killed and wounded, while his own loss was two killed and six wounded. Jones admits his casualties to have been seven killed and twenty-two wounded.

These delays enabled Federal reinforcements to be sent west over the Baltimore and Ohio Railroad, to points threatened by Imboden's strong column, before the raiding parties from Jones's command succeeded in interrupting rail communication at Oakland, but Jones afterwards passed one column of his troops through Oakland to Kingwood and thence to Morgantown on the Monongahela, during the 26th, while his main party went direct to Rowlesburg, at Cheat River Bridge on the railroad, by way of the Northwestern turnpike through West Union.

The column Jones sent to the railroad at Oakland also destroyed some small bridges farther east, at Altamont, stopping for a while traffic on that part of the line, but the party which went to Rowlesburg, April 26, to capture the small garrison there and then destroy the massive railroad viaduct and the trestle work nearby, failed in its attempt. Jones, with his main party, went as far as Evansville, where he found meat and forage, and endeavored to communicate with Imboden from whom he could get no news. Jones then crossed to the north of the railroad from Evansville, destroying a two-span bridge at Independence, and, on the 28th, having been joined by the column he had sent through Oakland, reached Morgantown, on the Monongahela, north of Grafton. He crossed to the west side of the river over the suspension bridge and then turned south on Fairmont and captured the garrison at that place on the 29th, by making a slight detour to the west. An unsuccessful effort to save the garrison and the railroad bridge was made by rail from Grafton, but came too late. Jones drove off this succoring party and then thoroughly destroyed the fine railroad bridge at Fairmont (on the Wheeling and Grafton branch of the Baltimore and Ohio Railroad). He sent a small party as far as Mannington.

During the night of the 29th and on the 30th, Jones continued his march southward from Fairmont, searching for Imboden but avoiding Clarksburg, where the Federal troops were in strength. He crossed to the south of the railroad at Bridgeport, five miles east of Clarksburg, capturing the small garrison there, consisting of 47 men, and destroyed the railroad bridge nearby, besides a railroad train which was run into Simpson's Creek. He reached Philippi at noon of May 1st, where he disencumbered himself of all impedimenta in the shape of captured animals, wagons, beef cattle, etc. These he sent to Beverly, under escort of the Sixth Virginia Cavalry, and with his main force moved leisurely to Buckhannon, where he found Imboden's command on the 2d of May, preparing to move on Weston, in which direction the joint command then marched. Their route was unobstructed except for the bad condition of the roads, as Gen. B. S. Roberts, in command of the Federal forces, had withdrawn to Clarksburg and Grafton all the small garrisons that had held Beverly, Philippi, Buckhannon and Weston, on Imboden's approach to those places, destroying vast quantities of stores, but still leaving much to fall into Imboden's hands.

Roberts was more apprehensive of the enemy under Jones getting possession of Clarksburg and Grafton, with all the military stores and railroad material accumulated there, than he was of attack from Imboden separately, but with a junction of Jones's and Imboden's two columns impending, with communication by rail already severed east and north by Jones's raid, thus cutting him off from all immediate reinforcement, Roberts very wisely decided to draw in to the railroad, at the two points above mentioned, all his scattered garrisons to the southward. This he succeeded in accomplishing by the 28th of April, he himself taking into Clarksburg everything from the Weston line that he did not destroy, while Colonel Mulligan retired into Grafton with the force from Philippi.

Imboden, after getting possession of Beverly, on the 24th of April, followed the retreating garrison a few miles toward Philippi and then discontinued the pursuit. He had previously secured possession of the direct road from Beverly to Buckhannon over Rich Mountain (the scene of General McClellan's brilliant operations in July, 1861), so that the Beverly garrison was forced to retreat on Buckhannon by a detour through Philippi, which it safely accomplished on the 26th, although Imboden had pushed out to the Buckhannon River, midway between Philippi and Buckhannon, but too late to intercept the movement.

Colonel Mulligan, the Federal commander at Grafton, having been reinforced from the east by two Maryland regiments from New Creek before Jones broke the railroad at Altamont and Oakland, and acting under instructions from General Roberts, had reoccupied Philippi on the 26th, when the Beverly garrison under Colonel Latham had already left for Buckhannon, Mulligan being sent to Philippi to help Latham's retirement; but finding Latham was safe and that Grafton was being threatened by Jones's troopers, Mulligan returned to Grafton on the 27th.

The country north of the Baltimore and Ohio Railroad in West Virginia, and even as far away as Harrisburg from the region being raided, was in an uproarious panic, which was greatly intensified by the telegraph operators along the railroad sending broadcast alarming messages concerning the raiders, before abandoning their posts. The commanding officer at Clarksburg, Col. N. Wilkinson, contributed no little to the panic by erroneously reporting to Roberts the capture of Grafton and Webster, and adding that he was preparing to abandon Clarksburg. Indeed, it was only after considerable urging that Roberts induced Wilkinson to hold on at Clarksburg until Roberts could reach there with the troops on the Buckhannon and Weston lines.

At Wheeling, on the 28th, the banks and the postal authorities were packing up their valuables ready for removal, while the United States Ordnance Officer stationed there asked for authority to "blow up the depot in case it is necessary" (meaning the Ordnance Depot). Jones was then at Morgantown, threatening Pittsburg as well as Wheeling, and his troops, 2,000 strong, were about to destroy the bridge at Fairmont, only twelve miles north of Grafton, on the railroad to Wheeling, besides sending a detachment to Mannington, only twelve miles from Wheeling. To intensify the situation, the commanding officer at Clarksburg, Colonel Wilkinson, had deemed it prudent two days before to destroy a bridge on the railroad five miles east of Clarksburg, thereby severing rail communication with Grafton and obstructing any reinforcement to Clarksburg from the East.

The enemy under Jones and Imboden, having joined their forces at Weston, on the 4th of May, and withdrawn their raiding parties from the Baltimore and Ohio Railroad east of Clarksburg, an attack on Clarksburg with the joint command, then about 6,000 strong, was contemplated, but abandoned when information had been received of the arrival there of material reinforcements from Harper's Ferry, Winchester and New Creek. It was decided, instead, that Imboden (whose troops were mostly dismounted) should move south, while Jones, with his cavalry, should raid the railroad west toward Parkersburg.

This latter movement was commenced on the 6th of May by sending the Eleventh and Twelfth Regiments and part of the Thirty-fourth Virginia Cavalry, all under Col. A. W. Harman (Twelfth Virginia Cavalry), to West Union, while, with the remainder of his command, Jones moved westward on the Parkersburg turnpike. Harman destroyed several small bridges on the railroad before reuniting with the main column under Jones at Cairo, where several more bridges were burned. From Cairo the command went to Oiltown, on the Little Kanawha, where, on the 9th of May, it destroyed the extensive oil-works and an immense quantity of the oil. From Oiltown Jones marched southeastward via Glenville and Sutton to Summerville, where he again rejoined Imboden on the 31st of May, and thence returned leisurely to the upper Shenandoah by way of the Greenbrier Valley. His losses were 10 killed, 42 wounded and 15 missing. He brought out 1,250 head of cattle and 1,200 horses, but was unencumbered by wagons during a march of about 700 miles. He claims to have killed about 25 of the enemy and wounded about 75, besides capturing about 700 prisoners with their small arms and one piece of artillery, two trains of cars, sixteen railroad bridges and a vast quantity of oil, with appurtenances, were burned. But he failed to destroy the Cheat River Viaduct, which was the main object of the expedition.

Imboden, after sending his sick and stores to Monterey by way of Beverly, had moved on the 6th south toward Summerville, over very bad roads daily made worse by the rains, passing through Bulltown and Suttonville. His advance guard, on the 12th of May, captured part of the rear guard and train of the Federal troops, six miles beyond Summerville, about two hours after they had evacuated the town.

From Summerville Imboden sent part of his force to cross the Gauley River at Hughes' Ferry and thence via Meadow Bluff to Lewisburg, while the main force marched up the Gauley and by the Cold Knob road, both parties eventually reaching Buffalo Gap near Staunton. Imboden's losses were only 16 men, besides about 200 deserters, but he recruited about 500 for his own and W. L. Jackson's regiments and brought out about $100,000 worth of captured horses, mules, wagons and arms, besides purchasing, in the country passed over, 3,100 head of fine cattle for the Commissary Department of the Confederate Army. The expectation that a considerable part of the people of West Virginia would flock to his flag was not realized.

While this double raid from the Shenandoah into West Virginia was occurring, Hooker's unsuccessful movement across the Rappahannock above Fredericksburg and the Battle of Chancellorsville (May 1, 2 and 3, 1863,) took place. In the latter battle the celebrated General (Stonewall) Jackson was mortally wounded, his death following a week later.

It had been Jackson's dream, since the beginning of hostilities, to lead an expedition to Clarksburg, W. Va., which had been his home in early life. On the day Jackson's final summons reached him (May 10) the Jones-Imboden raid to the vicinity of Clarksburg had become an accomplished fact.

To the comparatively small amount of damage done by Jones's and Imboden's raid into West Virginia, Stoneman's great and destructive cavalry raid to the vicinity of Gordonsville and Richmond, at about the same period, and his burning of railroad bridges as well as the commotion he caused, was more than an offset. It so disturbed General Lee that, in a letter of May 9th to Gen. Sam Jones, he says: "You see how General Stoneman has been running wild over the State, cutting our railroads, etc., and even going to within sight of Richmond. He must be restricted in his operations or we shall be ruined."

Had Hooker, with his still preponderating force, immediately renewed his attack on Lee at Fredericksburg, while Stoneman, with 28 regiments of cavalry, was operating well to the rear on Lee's communications, an important result might have been obtained.

CHAPTER VII

The Gettysburg Campaign and Second Battle of Winchester

On his return to the Shenandoah Valley, Gen. W. E. Jones's Brigade of Cavalry was ordered east of the Blue Ridge by General Lee, to join Gen. J. E. B. Stuart's cavalry command in the region of Culpeper Court-House. Gen, A. G. Jenkins's Brigade of Cavalry, from Gen. Sam Jones's Department of West Virginia, replaced W. E. Jones's Brigade in the Valley. In addition to Jenkins's cavalry, there were then in the upper Valley a battalion of Maryland cavalry and about a regiment of Maryland infantry, besides Imboden's Brigade of Partisan Rangers at Monterey and local garrisons of depot troops, these latter mainly at Staunton, the supply point. The aggregate strength of the troops in the Valley District May 30, 1863, was about 8,000, and Maj.-Gen. I. R. Trimble was assigned to command them.

The Federal troops, under Milroy, occupied Berryville, Winchester and Romney, with outposts toward Strasburg and Front Royal. Harper's Ferry and Maryland Heights, Martinsburg, Williamsport and posts westward to Cumberland and New Creek were held in strength by troops belonging to Gen. B. F. Kelley's command.

As early as May 19 General Lee commenced his preparations for his second invasion of Maryland, which culminated in the Battle of Gettysburg. He had been hampered by the difficulty of finding troops to meet the threatening Federal concentrations, not only in his own front on the Rappahannock but to meet the advance toward Richmond, south of the James from Suffolk as well as a concentration made at West Point, on York River.

Burnside, in Kentucky, was already at Somerset on the Cumberland River, having Knoxville as his objective, and the powerful army of Rosecrans at Murfreesborough, in Tennessee, was preparing to attack Bragg at Tullahoma and force its way toward Chattanooga. Then, too, General Grant had already commenced his Vicksburg campaign on the Mississippi, and on the South Atlantic coast troops were sorely needed to defend Charleston, Wilmington and intermediate points, so Lee could draw no reinforcements from these places.

It was to divert Federal attention, as well as to draw away Federal troops from the threatening movements above mentioned, that General Lee's second Maryland and the Gettysburg campaign were conceived, notwithstanding that General Hooker with a vastly superior force was immediately confronting him at Fredericksburg, the relative strength of the two armies being as 90,000 Confederates to over 100,000 Federals.

General Lee reorganized the infantry of his Army of Northern Virginia into three army corps instead of two, commanded respectively by Longstreet, Ewell and A. P. Hill. He had found that 30,000 men was too large a command for any corps commander to handle, especially when operating in broken countries. His cavalry, under J. E. B. Stuart, was also rearranged within brigades, these brigades being commanded as before by Wade Hampton, Fitzhugh Lee, W. H. F. "Rooney" Lee,[xiii] W. E. Jones; A. G. Jenkins's Brigade being on detached duty in the Valley of Virginia (the Shenandoah), and Robertson's Brigade still in North Carolina. The artillery, which was organized by battalions and counted altogether 270 guns, was assigned by battalions, to the three army corps, each battalion consisting of four batteries, usually of four guns each. This gave each division of the three army corps a battalion of artillery, with an artillery reserve of two battalions to each corps.

During the latter part of May information came to the Federal authorities that General Lee was undoubtedly preparing for some aggressive movement, indications being that it would consist, first, of turning General Hooker's right flank by way of the Upper Rappahannock. These rumors were confirmed when Stuart's Cavalry, covering Ewell's and Longstreet's Corps, advanced on the 7th of June from the region of Culpeper Court-House toward the Rappahannock at Beverly Ford and above.

Ewell's Corps had previously been moved, on the 4th of June, from Hamilton's Crossing, of the Rappahannock, below Fredericksburg, across country, via Verdierville and Somerville Ford, of the Rapidan, to Culpeper, which was reached on the 7th of June. Longstreet's Corps had been moved also to Culpeper from Fredericksburg on the 3d of June. Stuart's Cavalry had then been pushed out toward the Upper Rappahannock from the vicinity of Culpeper. Stuart was attacked by all of Hooker's Cavalry, under Gen. Alfred Pleasanton, supported by about 1,500 infantry, the two columns under Pleasanton having crossed the Rappahannock, on the 9th of June, at Beverly and Kelly's Fords, and converged toward Brandy Station of the Orange and Alexandria Railroad.

From this reconnaissance ensued the brilliant cavalry engagement, on the 9th, known by the Confederates as the Battle of Fleetwood and by the Federal troops as that of Beverly Ford. The movement developed the fact that the Confederates were in very heavy force beyond Hooker's right flank, south of the Rappahannock, and, from papers captured in Stuart's camp, that Stuart was to have started on a g-aid into Maryland that very day, June 9th, but that expedition was then deferred until later.

Enough was ascertained of the enemy's movements, however, to cause Hooker at once to move the bulk of his army from in front of Fredericksburg toward his right, up the north bank of the Rappahannock, so as to be prepared to cover Washington while operating on an interior line to that of the enemy, should the latter intend another invasion of Maryland by way of the upper Potomac.

General Lee, who had already moved his headquarters to Culpeper, from which point he was watching the effect on Hooker's forces of the withdrawal of two of his three army corps from Fredericksburg, had determined on the 7th of June to commence that part of his projected movement which embraced the clearing of a way through the lower Shenandoah Valley, by forcing out of Winchester and Berryville the troops then in occupation, under Milroy.

Accordingly, on the 7th of June, he sent orders to Imboden, then near Monterey with his Partisan Ranger Brigade, to move on Romney, by way of the South Branch of the Potomac, through Franklin and Moorefield On the same day he sent orders to Gen. A. G. Jenkins, with his brigade of regular cavalry, to move down the Valley of the Shenandoah and "to be concentrated at Strasburg or Front Royal, or any point in front of either, by Wednesday, the 10th instant, with a view to cooperate with a force of infantry. Your pickets can be kept in advance as far as you may deem best toward Winchester."

Imboden's movement was intended mainly "to attract the enemy's attention in Hampshire County and to detain "whatever force they may have at New Creek, Cumberland, Cacapon, etc."; but Imboden's general instructions were: "Of course, do them all the injury in your power, by striking them a damaging blow at any point where opportunity offers, and where you deem most practicable. It will be important, if you can accomplish it, to destroy some of the bridges, so as to prevent communication and the transfer of reinforcements to Martinsburg." Imboden, with his force of 2,500 men, was then to "cooperate with any troops that he might find operating in the Shenandoah Valley"; he was also "to collect in the country passed through all the cattle and recruits possible." General Lee had kept Imboden's brigade of partisans independent of all other commands and had him report directly to himself (General Lee) for orders. Imboden's command was made up mainly of mountaineers recruited in the Alleghenies, thoroughly familiar with every valley, stream or cattle track. Moreover, under the Confederate Partisan Ranger Act of April 21, 1862, they enjoyed immunity from the treatment usually accorded the ordinary guerilla, and, besides, were given a bonus for all property (munitions of war) captured by them and turned over to the regularly constituted Confederate agents. Their loyalty and zeal were thus doubly stimulated.

The day following the cavalry engagement at Beverly Ford of the Upper Rappahannock, Ewell's Corps was set in motion from near Culpeper for the Shenandoah, moving via Gaines's Cross-Roads, Flint Hill and Front Royal, reaching Cedarville in the Valley on the 12th of June. There, on the 13th, Ewell detached Rodes's Division, with Jenkin's Cavalry Brigade, to move on Berryville and endeavor to capture McReynolds's Brigade of Milroy's Division, about 2,000 strong, which had been in position there for several months, but McReynolds made good his retirement on Winchester where he joined Milroy's main force.

Ewell sent Early's Division toward Winchester via Newtown and the Valley turnpike, while Edward Johnson's Division moved upon Winchester by the direct road from Front Royal. The three divisions were all in position before Winchester on the morning of June 14. Part of the outer works on the west side of the town, near the Pughtown road, were captured by some of Early's troops late in the afternoon and the main works thereby rendered untenable by Milroy's forces, who, during the night, endeavored to retire on Martinsburg. This, Ewell claims to have foreseen and provided against, by sending Johnson's Division late in the evening to place himself on the Martinsburg turnpike about two and a half miles north of Winchester, but Johnson could not reach the position assigned him until after Milroy's retreat had commenced, and when Milroy endeavored to cut through, the head of Johnson's column, near the Martinsburg pike, was ready to receive him and fired into Milroy's right flank, eventually throwing him into confusion. General Milroy, with a small party only, succeeded in reaching Harper's Ferry, although many other small parties of fugitives reached that place the following day.

By the abandonment of Winchester on the night of June 14, twenty-three pieces of artillery, 4,000 prisoners, 300 loaded wagons, more than 300 horses and a quantity of stores fell into the hands of the Confederates; their loss was 47 killed, 219 wounded, and 3 missing. Anticipating some such disaster, General Halleck from Washington had on the 11th of June, as soon as General Lee's threatened movement into "the Shenandoah Valley became probable, ordered Gen. Robert C. Schenck at Baltimore, to withdraw General Milroy's command from Winchester to Harper's Ferry, but the order had not been carried out when Ewell attacked there.

Although Rodes's Division of Ewell's Corps met some little resistance to his movement on Berryville, the troops of McReynolds's Federal Brigade succeeded in reaching Winchester by a roundabout way, safely, on the 13th. Rodes then moved on Martinsburg, sending Jenkins's cavalry through Bunker Hill. Martinsburg was evacuated during the evening of the 14th, the Federal infantry troops retiring unmolested toward Shepherdstown and Harper's Ferry, while the artillery, with a small infantry support, endeavored to reach Williamsport, but lost in the attempt five out of six guns and about 200 prisoners. On the 15th Rodes had crossed his three brigades at Williamsport and had sent Jenkins's Cavalry Brigade forward toward Chambersburg. On the 19th Rodes moved to Hagerstown and went into camp on the Boonsborough road, while Johnson crossed to Sharpsburg and Early moved from Winchester to Shepherdstown, to threaten Harper's Ferry, which still held out. Otherwise, the entire Shenandoah was once more in possession of the Confederates.

It was peculiarly fitting that General Lee should have entrusted to Ewell's Corps (formerly Jackson's) the recovery of that section of country, for the year previous Ewell had operated with Stonewall Jackson by way of Front Royal on Winchester, Martinsburg and Harper's Ferry, and he, as well as his troops, was thoroughly familiar with the terrain.

The cooperation of Imboden, by way of the valley of the South Branch of the Potomac, through Franklin, Moorefield and Romney, was also very fruitful of results and proved to be an invaluable flanking party to Ewell's more serious column. On the 18th of June Imboden reported to General Lee from French's Depot, on the Baltimore and Ohio Railroad, that he had destroyed all the important bridges on that railroad, with water tanks, depots and engines, between the Little Cacapon River and Cumberland. Also that he had collected and sent back a large quantity of horses and cattle. General Lee then authorized Imboden to move north on the left flank of Ewell's Corps.

General Lee, on the 16th, had moved his own headquarters from Culpeper to Millwood, near Winchester, and then to Berryville, where he perfected the subsequent movements of his army into Maryland and Pennsylvania. He maintained communication with Richmond by way of the Valley to Staunton and thence via Gordonsville.

Longstreet's Corps was put in motion from Culpeper toward Winchester via Front Royal on the 15th, and A. P. Hill's Corps was all withdrawn from Fredericksburg by the 17th, as soon as it was definitely ascertained that Hooker's entire army had been marched away from that front and that Richmond was no longer threatened from that direction. Hill moved across country by way of Germanna Ford of the Rapidan to Culpeper and thence followed the route of Longstreet's Corps.

Stuart's cavalry moved on the right flank of Longstreet's column, effectually screening the latter's movements, being repeatedly required to repel the enterprising efforts of Pleasanton's Federal cavalry from penetrating to the passes of the Blue Ridge at Ashby's and Snicker's Gaps, which Longstreet held. Spirited cavalry fighting occurred at Aldie, Middleburg and Upperville on the 17th, 19th and 21st of June, both bodies of cavalry being engaged in masking the location of their respective main armies, in which for several days each was very successful. Stuart was eventually forced back beyond Upperville and into Ashby's Gap.

On the 16th of June Hooker had his own headquarters at Fairfax Station, and concentrated his entire army near the old Bull Run battlefields, at Manassas, Centreville and Fairfax Court-House. It was Lee's announced intention to attack Hooker in case he took up any faulty position after being drawn away from the line of the Rappahannock, and, with this in view, Stuart's cavalry, supported by Longstreet's infantry, was specially zealous in his efforts to develop Hooker's whereabouts. .

At Harper's Ferry, on the 15th of June, were concentrated the remnants of Milroy's Division from Berryville and Winchester, Tyler's Brigade from Martinsburg, and the original garrison of Harper's Ferry, in all a force of about 6,000 men, which was placed mainly upon Maryland Heights, on the north bank of the Potomac, a strong grand guard only occupying the town. The whole was placed under the command of Gen. Dan Tyler, Milroy being relieved for his delay in leaving Winchester and for the disaster to his command which thereby ensued. Milroy's conduct was soon afterwards investigated by a court of inquiry, which acquitted Milroy of all blame, as his immediate commander, Gen. R. C. Schenck, had authorized Milroy only to prepare to evacuate but to then await further orders, which never came.

With the capture of Winchester and the appearance of so large a portion of Lee's army north of the Potomac, at Williamsport and beyond, any doubts that may have remained of Lee's intentions were dispelled from the minds of President Lincoln and his advisers. At this time the relations between General Hooker and the General-in-Chief of the Army (General Halleck) had become so strained that the former never communicated with the latter if he could avoid it. In a dispatch to the President of June 16th, 11 A. M., Hooker says: "You have long been aware, Mr. President, that I have not enjoyed the confidence of the Major-General commanding the army, and I assure you so long as this continues we may look in vain for success, especially as future operations will require our relations to be more dependent upon each other than heretofore."

At 10 p. M. that same night (June 16) Mr. Lincoln telegraphed General Hooker: "To remove all misunderstanding, I now place you in the strict military relation to General Halleck of a commander of one of the armies to the General-in-Chief of all the armies. I have not intended differently, but as it seems to be differently understood, I shall direct him to give you orders and you to obey them."

Almost simultaneously, at 10.15 p. m. General Halleck directed General Hooker to move a strong column of his army to Leesburg, "to ascertain where the enemy is and then move to the relief of Harper's Ferry, or elsewhere, as circumstances might require. With the remainder of your force in proper position to support this, I want you to push your cavalry to ascertain something definite about the enemy."

It has been seen that Hooker's cavalry was already in motion to endeavor to locate Lee's main army, and that it became hotly engaged with the Confederate cavalry at Aldie, on the 17th, but could not penetrate the screen sufficiently far to develop the infantry supports of Longstreet's Corps, then holding the passes of the Blue Ridge. On that date Tyler, with about 10,000 men, was on Maryland Heights, opposite Harper's

Ferry, unmolested, although threatened by Ewell's Corps and Jenkins's cavalry, which had crossed the Potomac northwest of him two days before. On the 17th, also, the Twelfth Corps of Hooker's Army, under Slocum, was put in motion for Leesburg, the remainder of his army being strung out on a line that passed through Gum Springs, Centreville, and Sangster's Station. In the absence of definite information of the whereabouts of Lee's main army or of the latter's intentions, it was not deemed prudent either by General Halleck or by General Hooker to move any portion of the Army of the Potomac north into Maryland, and it was only on the 25th, when Lee's undoubted movement on Harrisburg became confirmed, for all his infantry had then crossed the Potomac, that Hooker's army was also moved across the Potomac at Leesburg and Edward's Ferry in pursuit of Lee. At Poolesville, in Maryland, on the 25th of June, General Hooker reported his strength at 105,000 men. On the 27th he requested to be relieved of the command of the Army of the Potomac, owing to a new disagreement with General Halleck. His request was complied with at once and Gen. George G. Meade designated as his successor. Under the latter the Army of the Potomac was marched to Gettysburg, where Lee had concentrated his army, and where was fought what is considered the bloodiest battle of the war, resulting in Lee's defeat and the retreat of his army back to the south side of the Potomac at Falling Waters, which was safely accomplished on the 14th of July.

On leaving Winchester to move into Maryland, on the 18th of June, Early left the Thirteenth Virginia Infantry to garrison the town, having previously sent the Fifty-fourth North Carolina and the Fifty-eighth Virginia back to Staunton to escort the prisoners, about 3,000 in number, taken from Milroy and Tyler.

On the 16th of July, after his return from Pennsylvania, Lee's army was encamped around Bunker Hill, Va., between Winchester and Harper's Ferry. He reported to President Davis he did not need any more troops, and recommended that such as had been collected be kept in front of Richmond as a protection to that city. Lee also wrote: "I learn the enemy has thrown a pontoon bridge over the Potomac at Harper's Ferry. Should he follow us in this direction, I shall lead him up the Valley, and endeavor to attack him as far from his base as possible.

From Culpeper, on the 24th of July, General Lee reported that his intention had been to move his army into Loudoun County, but the high water in the Shenandoah River had first prevented that movement and then the enemy had occupied in such strong force the passes of the Blue Ridge that they could not easily be forced, and, besides, he threatened a movement on Richmond. This determined Lee to move up the Valley and cross the Blue Ridge at Chester's and Thornton's Gaps.

While threatened by Meade's main army on one flank from the Blue Ridge, Lee had also been more or less annoyed by the Federal forces sent after him by way of Harper's Ferry, and by a column which Gen. B. F. Kelley had hastily gathered in West Virginia, and had moved via Hancock, where he crossed the Potomac, on Lee's 'other flank. At Hedgesville, on the 19th of July, Kelley had a brisk engagement with some of the enemy's forces holding Martinsburg; he reoccupied Martinsburg with Averell's Brigade on the 25th and Winchester on the 26th.

Gen. John D. Imboden, on the 21st of July, had been assigned to command the Valley District by Lee, in recognition of his valuable services during the Gettysburg campaign and because of his great familiarity with the country. His troops consisted of his own partisan brigade of infantry, cavalry and artillery, known as the Northwestern Brigade and numbering about 2,500 men. His headquarters were in the upper Valley. General Lee's instructions to Imboden were to be vigilant and to seize every opportunity to strike the enemy a blow, "and annoy him all in your power." On the 26th of July Imboden was near Woodstock with his command, when he was urged by General Lee to make "a rapid movement upon Piedmont or some point higher up the railroad." Imboden undertook the above-mentioned raid in September, of which mention will be made later on.

Averell had moved his brigade away from Winchester altogether, on the 5th of August, to Moorefield via Wardensville, and to the Upper Valley of the South Branch of the Potomac, on an expedition toward

Lewisburg which finally reached the vicinity of White Sulphur Springs, in Greenbrier County, where, at Rocky Gap, on the 26th of August, Averell met a force under Gen. Echols, of Gen. Sam Jones's command, too strong for him to drive out, and which forced him to retire through Huntersville to Beverly, where he arrived and took station on the 31st of August. He was again within the limits of the territory assigned him to command.

Winchester was not then reoccupied in force by Federal troops, being only visited occasionally by patrols sent out from Harper's Ferry or Martinsburg. At Harper's Ferry there was a force of 5,500 men under Gen. Henry H. Lockwood. A brigade under McReynolds was stationed at Martinsburg, and a brigade under Col. J. A. Mulligan was sent from New Creek to occupy Moorefield and Petersburg, in the South Potomac Valley, after Averell had passed south, as an outpost from New Creek on the Baltimore and Ohio Railroad. A small force was also posted by General Kelley at Romney, 27 miles down the South Branch of the Potomac from Moorefield.

The Department of West Virginia, commanded by Gen. B. F. Kelley, had been extended on the 9th of August so as to include all the State of Maryland west of the Monocacy River, and that portion of Virginia in the vicinity of Harper's Ferry. By the tri-monthly return of August 10, 1863, the troops therein numbered 18,114 present for duty, soon afterwards increased to nearly 30,000. These were distributed as follows:

Maryland Heights Division, 5,000; Martinsburg, 3,000; Sir John's Run and Romney, 1,000; New Creek (Keyser), 3,000; Petersburg, 3,000; Grafton and Parkersburg, 3,000; Kanawha, 6,000; Beverly, 4,000, and several small scattered commands. The Baltimore and Ohio Railroad were thus securely guarded throughout its entire length, and direct communication maintained with the West.

This was a period of great depression in the North as well as at the South. Following Lee's defeat at Gettysburg, in July, and his escape back to his old position, near Culpeper, came the draft riots in New York and the necessary detachment of a large force from Meade's army to quell them. For the time being all eyes were then turned toward East Tennessee, where Burnside had succeeded in reaching and establishing himself at Knoxville, while Rosecrans, moving on Burnside's flank farther west, had crossed the Tennessee River, and was seeking to gain possession of Chattanooga. To arrest the progress of Rosecrans, Lee detached from his army Longstreet's entire Army Corps, and hurried it by rail through North Carolina and Atlanta to reinforce Bragg's army in Northern Georgia.

All the Confederate armies had become greatly weakened by the enormous losses incident to the campaigns and battles of the preceding two years, to which should be added the appalling number of desertions of those whom the terrible experiences of the war had disheartened. It had already become almost entirely impossible to procure recruits, even by the extraordinary methods of conscription, the age limit even being extended so as to take in boys of eighteen and men of forty-five.

In the hope that many of those hiding in desertion might be induced to return to the ranks, President Davis, in August, proclaimed amnesty to such as would rejoin within twenty days, the women of the Confederacy being conjured to use their all-powerful influence to aid the measure. Meanwhile, patrols were actively searching every possible hiding place of those recreant, but generally meeting armed resistance.

General Lee himself, in a letter to President Davis from Orange Court-House, August 8, gives the following despondent view of the situation: "We must expect reverses, even defeats. They are sent to teach us wisdom and prudence. I know how prone we are to censure and how ready to blame others for the non-fulfillment of our expectations. This is unbecoming in a generous people, and I grieve to see its expression. The general remedy for the want of success in a military commander is his removal. This is natural, and, in many instances, proper. I have been prompted by these reflections more than once since my return from Pennsylvania to propose to Your Excellency the propriety of selecting another commander for this army. I have seen and heard expression of discontent in the public journals as the result of the expedition. I do not know how far this feeling extends to the army. I, therefore, in all sincerity, request Your Excellency to take measures to supply my place. I hope Your Excellency will attribute my request to the true reason, the desire to serve my country, and to do all in my power to insure the success of her righteous cause."

This request of General Lee, however, was never granted.

At the North, also, great dissatisfaction had been expressed in the newspapers at General Meade's failure to attack and destroy Lee's army when he found it still north of the Potomac, ten days after the Battle of Gettysburg, and trying to cross that swollen river in the vicinity of Williamsport. The explanation made by General Meade, why Lee was not attacked in his perilous position, apparently satisfied the Washington authorities, for Meade was continued in command of the Army of the Potomac until the close of the war. When General Grant was brought from the Middle West, in March, 1864, and placed in command of all the armies in the field, he selected the Army of the Potomac to supervise in particular.

CHAPTER VIII
The Averell Raids of 1863

With a view to carrying out General Lee's instructions "to seize every opportunity to strike the enemy a blow and annoy him all in your power," Imboden, on the 13th of September, 1863, from near Brock's Gap in the upper Valley, reported several minor engagements of his Rangers in the Valley District, which included a foray through Winchester to Bath (Berkeley Springs) on the 6th, killing, wounding and capturing part of Wynkoop's Pennsylvania Cavalry at the latter place. Also an affair between four companies of Imboden's cavalry and a small force of Federal infantry and cavalry, on the 11th, near Moorefield, killing and capturing, with small loss, about 150 of the latter by surprise. Imboden stated: "I am so well convinced of the utility of this mode of warfare on the border, that day after to-morrow I start out two parties, one of 100 men under Major Lang, Sixty-second Virginia Regiment, to penetrate the enemy's country north of Beverly on foot, and harass the enemy two or three weeks in Barbour and Randolph; the other, a single company, under Captain Nelson, to go to the North Fork, in Pendleton, and try to clear out Snyder's gang of Union robbers and murderers, known as 'Swamp Dragoons.' All remains quiet in the lower Valley. Only a small force of the enemy at Martinsburg and Harper's Ferry, and they stick to the railroad very closely."

The most serious of these small affairs was the capture of 356 officers and men, mostly of the Ninth Maryland Infantry (Colonel Simpson), at Charlestown, ten miles southwest of Harper's Ferry, on the 18th of October, by a force of about 1,500 men belonging to Imboden's, Gilmor's and "White's commands, with artillery. This Confederate party was in turn attacked by a force, sent out from Harper's Ferry by Gen. Jer. C. Sullivan, who had succeeded to that command when General Lockwood was relieved. Imboden was driven through Charlestown to near Berryville, the Federals capturing twenty-one prisoners and killing or wounding about as many more.

This movement by Imboden was in pursuance of orders sent him by General Lee on the 9th of October, when Lee commenced his flanking march around Meade's army at Culpeper, and which forced the latter to retire north of Bull Run. Lee in his report, dated October 23, says: "General Imboden[xiv] was instructed to advance down the Valley and guard the gaps on our left."

Imboden fell back from Berryville, first, to Front Royal, and then to the upper Valley by way of Powell's Fort Valley, to meet an expected expedition under Averell, which was reported to be forming near Huttonsville, in Tygart's River Valley, west of the main Alleghenies, and threatening to move either upon Staunton or Lewisburg.

This movement was started by Averell, by orders from Gen. B. F. Kelley, on the 1st of November, and proceeded over Cheat Mountain into the Valley of the Greenbrier, via Camp Bartow, to Huntersville, which it reached on the 4th. It consisted of Averell's entire brigade, except about 400 men, left to hold Beverly; about half of it was mounted infantry. Averell attacked the Confederates under Gen. John Echols on Droop Mountain, twenty miles north of Lewisburg, on the 6th, completely defeating him and driving him out in the direction of Lewisburg, where Averell followed him through the town on the 7th, Echols's men retreating toward Union and the narrows of New River, blockading the roads behind them.

On reaching Lewisburg, Averell found Duffié 's Federal cavalry brigade, which had just arrived from Meadow Bluff and the Kanawha to the westward, but not in time to intercept the Confederate fugitives from Droop Mountain. Averell's instructions from Kelley contemplated a further movement from Lewisburg toward the Virginia and Tennessee Railroad at Dublin, to destroy an important bridge at that point, but discretion was left to Averell as to that further movement after he should have reached Lewisburg and been joined there by Duffié .

On the 8th, Averell, with Duffié, again pushed forward toward Dublin via Union, but after going a few miles he found the road so formidably blockaded that it was necessary to cut out a passage. Here General Duffié reported his men as being unfit for further operations, having only one day's rations left and so exhausted as to be able to march only ten miles per day. This decided Averell to abandon further pursuit of Echols and to send Duffié back to Meadow Bluff, while he (Averell) should send his dismounted troops (two regiments) and one battery back to Beverly, escorting the prisoners, captured property, etc. With his mounted troops, Averell then proceeded to carry out the remainder of Kelley's instructions, which were to "move by any route you may think best, into the Valley of the South Branch (of the Potomac), and down that to New Creek, where supplies will be in readiness for you."

Accordingly, with his mounted troops (four regiments) and Ewing's Battery, Averell marched through White Sulphur Springs and the August battle-ground of Dry Creek (Rocky Gap), picking up his wounded who had been cared for by the Confederates since August, and reached Callaghan's, on the road to Covington, early on the 9th of November. He was then on the east side of the main Allegheny Mountains. Learning that Imboden, with a small force of about 1,500 men, was at Covington, he sent a small mounted party to brush him away from his line of march, capturing a few prisoners.

From Callaghan's the march northward was continued by Gatewood's into the Valley of Back Creek (a branch of Jackson's River), thence up that stream and through Hightown and Monterey to Franklin, in the South Branch Valley, and to Petersburg, which latter place was reached on the 13th and supplies found for the command. On the 17th Averell arrived at New Creek (Keyser), bringing with him about 150 captured horses, several hundred head of cattle and 27 prisoners, taken in addition to those already sent to Beverly. Averell's losses at Droop Mountain aggregated 119 killed, wounded and missing; those of the enemy, as stated by General Echols, were 275.

The part taken by Imboden in the foregoing operations was important only as one of observation. He was at Goshen, on the railroad, a few miles west of Staunton, on the 6th of November, with most of his command, and at Covington on the 8th; from there he returned to Goshen via Clifton Forge on the 10th and to Buffalo Gap, near Staunton, on the 11th, which place he feared might receive a visit from Averell by way of Monterey. That not coming off, Imboden moved his command farther down the Valley to near Mount Jackson, sending occasional scouting parties toward Berryville, Strasburg, and Moorefield.

Having rested and refitted his brigade at New Creek (Keyser) since his arrival there, on the 17th of November, General Averell started out again on another expedition into the enemy's country on the 8th of December. His general instructions from Gen. B. F. Kelley, commanding the Department of West Virginia, were to proceed via Petersburg, Franklin and Monterey, by the most practicable route to the line of the Virginia and Tennessee Railroad at Bonsack's Station, in Botetourt County, or Salem, in Roanoke County, or, by dividing his command, move on both points at the same time. The object was to destroy or cripple that railroad. At Petersburg, Averell was to pick up two regiments of infantry and a battery belonging to Thoburn's Brigade, carrying them with him as far as Monterey, at the head of the South Branch Valley, where he was to leave them to guard his train and await his return. Having accomplished the object of his expedition, Averell was to return to the Baltimore and Ohio Railroad, at any point he might deem best, between Harper's Ferry and New Creek.

After receiving these orders, Averell secured from General Kelley several modifications of them, which proved of great value as cooperations or diversions. One was that, simultaneously with his own movement, Scammon should move his forces in the Kanawha region eastward to Lewisburg, as a protection against any forces of the enemy coming in from the north, and then to operate to the southward, on Union or beyond. The date fixed for Scammon to be at Lewisburg was December 12th, and he was to remain in that vicinity until the 18th.

Moor's Brigade was to move forward from Beverly toward Droop Mountain, reaching that vicinity also on the 12th, and to remain until the 18th, when he was to withdraw, bringing off the wounded left behind near there after the battle of the 6th November.

Sullivan's Division, at Harper's Ferry, was to move up to Woodstock, in the Valley, so as to get there by the 12th of December, and remain near there until the

18th, when he was to move still farther toward Staunton and threaten that place, in cooperation with Thoburn's forces from the direction of Monterey.

It will thus be seen that all of General Kelley's troops were intended to be in motion toward a common center simultaneously, except those guarding the railroad at and west of Grafton.

Averell's own brigade was essentially a flying column, being composed of the Second, Third and Eighth West Virginia Mounted Infantry, Fourteenth Pennsylvania Cavalry, Gibson's Battalion of Cavalry and Ewing's Light Battery. He and Thoburn reached Monterey on the 12th, where Thoburn, with all the wagons except about forty, was sent to McDowell, on the Parkersburg road to Staunton, while Averell with his flying column and the forty wagons proceeded down Back Creek, a fork of Jackson's River, where, at Gatewood's, on the 13th, he came upon the rear-guard of W. L. Jackson's regiment (the Nineteenth Virginia) retreating from the Greenbrier country, west of the mountains, whence they had been driven out by Moor's Brigade from Beverly, as intended they should be.

Pushing on to Callaghan's, which he reached on the 14th, Averell got information that Scammon had carried out his part of the general movement and was at Lewisburg, whence he had driven the Confederates, under Echols, and who were then retreating on Union and the Narrows of New River.

Early on the 15th of December Averell made a demonstration toward Covington as a feint to cover his main movement toward Salem, on the Virginia and Tennessee Railroad, by way of Sweet Sulphur Springs and New Castle. Salem was reached early on the 16th, just in time to partially tear up the railroad near the depot before a train loaded with troops approached from the direction of Lynchburg, which, by a few well-directed artillery shots, was forced to run back again. Parties were then sent out by Averell several miles to the eastward and westward to more thoroughly destroy the railroad, while everything that could be of value to the enemy in the vicinity of Salem was destroyed during the next six hours, when the command withdrew about seven miles on the New Castle road, by which it had come, and went into camp after a march of about 80 miles in 30 hours. A heavy rain then came up which made the return to New Castle very dangerous as well as difficult in the swollen creek bottoms, so that it was sundown of the 18th when New Castle was reached, and, as Averell says, with ammunition wet and the command "drenched, muddy and hungry in miserable condition to make the march before us."

At New Castle, Averell learned that Fitzhugh Lee, with his own and Imboden's troops, besides some cadets and militia from Lexington, Va., was near Fincastle, a few miles east of New Castle, and that Sam Jones, with troops from Union, was on the Sweet Springs road, north and west of him. With his ammunition virtually destroyed by the recent storms, Averell realized the necessity of avoiding a battle with either of the enemy's converging columns, so he determined to retreat to Covington in a northeasterly direction, which he succeeded in doing, although with some slight opposition from a mounted force of Confederates when still eight miles from Jackson's River. A captured dispatch of the 19th from Gen. Sam Jones to General Early, the latter being then at Millborough on the railroad between Covington and Staunton, informed Averell of the large force that had been sent by General Lee to intercept him, in addition to W. L. Jackson's command at Clifton Forge and Fitzhugh Lee's forces, above mentioned.

Averell succeeded in getting all his command, except one regiment and his small wagon train, across Jackson's River and through Covington during the night of the 19th, although sharply attacked by Jackson's troops in their efforts to destroy the bridges and thus cut him off. This isolated regiment (the Fourteenth Pennsylvania Cavalry) forded the river the following day, losing, however, over 120 prisoners and several men drowned, besides all the wagons and ambulances, but rejoined Averell at Callaghan's.

By following the very blind and seldom-used Cold Knob road, Averell then took his command over the main Allegheny Mountains and across the Greenbrier Valley to the northern slope of Droop Mountain, where he encamped on the night of the 21st, successfully avoiding contact with the advanced parties of Ewell's column, then reported to be at Gatewood's, only twenty miles to the eastward. At Droop Mountain, Averell expected to hear of Colonel Moor's command, which he had ordered to remain there until the 18th before withdrawing, but who had retired on the 14th by General Kelley's order. So Averell pushed on for Edray and Beverly with his very tired command of 2,500 men, over execrable roads, but unmolested by any enemy except a slight rear-guard action near Edray on the 22d. He reached Beverly safely on the 24th of December, having marched over 400 miles.

The country passed through by Averell is the most broken and mountainous of any in the Eastern United States, and the difficulty of campaigning in it can only be appreciated by a visit.

The valleys run nearly north and south, enclosed on the east and west by superb mountain ranges, most entrancing in summer but very forbidding in winter. The large streams become torrents in the rainy season, when wagoning is both difficult and hazardous. The bottom lands are very fertile and furnish large crops, while cattle, sheep and horses are abundant.

As above mentioned, Scammon with the Kanawha troops left Lewisburg sooner than Averell expected, and while he was still far within the enemy's country at Salem with his flying column, beyond all possible support. This left the enemy free to act from the direction of Union. Colonel Moor, who was to remain near Droop Mountain and Frankford until the 18th of December, was withdrawn several days before that date. Thoburn, with 700 men, who had been detached at

Monterey on the 12th and sent toward McDowell and Staunton on the Parkersburg pike to attract the enemy's attention from Averell's main movement, after accomplishing that mission returned to his station at Petersburg. The force sent directly up the Shenandoah Valley from Sullivan's command at Harper's Ferry went as far as Harrisonburg, threatening Staunton, 25 miles farther to the southward, and for a few days held the attention of Imboden's forces, as well as Early's and Fitzhugh Lee's, from Averell's movements on Salem. The enemy attempted to cut off this detachment by sending Colonel Rosser from Lee's army with a brigade of cavalry to fall upon its rear by way of Front Royal, but could not cross the Shenandoah River by reason of high water. Sullivan's detachment returned to Charlestown and Harper's Ferry on the 24th of December, the same day that Averell reached Beverly. Early, with his two brigades of infantry and Lee's two brigades of cavalry, having given up all hope of intercepting Averell's retreat, followed Sullivan's troops down the Valley through Harrisonburg to New Market, at which latter place, on the 24th of December, Early reported to General Lee the failure of all the Confederate columns, about 15,000 men in all, to head off or get contact with Averell. On this report Gen. R. E. Lee endorsed: "High water and erroneous reports, with untoward events, prevented the success of the arrangements that I had hoped would have resulted in Averell's capture."

After a short rest at Beverly, Averell marched his brigade to Webster via Philippi, where he put it on the cars and moved to Martinsburg, which place he reached on the 31st of December, 1863, just in time to prepare for the enemy under Imboden, Fitzhugh Lee and Rosser, who were demonstrating from the direction of Winchester to cover a movement the last two named were making on Moorefield and Petersburg by way of Wardensville, which was eventually extended to the vicinity of New Creek and the railroads but this movement failed of success on account of the high streams and the bitterly cold weather, so that Lee returned to Harrisonburg via Romney, Lost River and Brock's Gap. The only success Lee had was the capture of a small wagon train of artillery ammunition, about 100 prisoners and as many cattle. He reported there were very few supplies to be found in the region passed over, as it had long been occupied by an enemy.

With the appearance of Early's forces in the lower Valley, a brigade of infantry was sent from General Meade's army to strengthen the troops holding points between Harper's Ferry and Cumberland.

A new epoch may then be stated to have taken place in the Valley, commencing with Gen. Jubal A. Early's being placed in command there at the beginning of Averell's third raid and dating from December 15, 1863, when, by S. O. 308, Headquarters Army of Northern Virginia, General Lee directed Early to "proceed to Staunton, Va., and assume command of all the troops there and in the Valley of Virginia, and make the best disposition of the same to resist the advance of the enemy." This order, of course, was primarily to protect Staunton, with its extensive military depots, from the raiders under Averell or his cooperators. When that raid ended and the Upper Shenandoah region had been cleared of Federal troops, General Lee, under date of December 22, 1863, wrote General Early, then at New Market, as follows:

"I wish you to avail yourself of the present opportunity to collect and bring away everything that can be made useful to the army from those regions that are open to the enemy. I hear that in the lower Valley, and particularly in the country on the South Branch of the Potomac, there are a good many cattle, sheep, horses and hogs, and all these supplies are accessible to and can be used by the enemy. I desire to secure all of them that it is in our power to get, and you will use your command for the purpose of keeping back the enemy while the work is being done. Where you cannot buy, you must impress. Of course, you will not take what is necessary for the subsistence of the people, but leave enough for that. While so engaged, I wish you to subsist the troops on those supplies that are most difficult of transportation, such as bacon, potatoes, and other vegetables, sending back those that are easy to transport, such as cattle, particularly sheep and hogs. "P. S.—You will give out that your movement is intended as a military one against the enemy, and, of course, will do them all the harm you can. You will use all the troops, including those of Imboden and Gilmor that you may require."

At this time all the Confederate armies were in sore straits for subsistence. So much so that, most reluctantly, resort was had to impressment where purchases were impossible, mainly by reason of prohibitive prices. This impressment was made under the provisions of the Act of March 26, 1863, and its subsequent amendments.

Early's force in the Valley consisted of two brigades of infantry (H. H. Walker's and Thomas's) from his old division in Ewell's Corps; Imboden's Brigade of Partisans; Gilmor's and White's Battalions (also partisans); W. L. Jackson's Brigade of Infantry; some artillery and Rosser's Brigade of Cavalry. The remainder of Fitzhugh Lee's Cavalry Division was withdrawn to Charlottesville during the latter part of January, 1864.

Throughout the winter and spring of 1864 Early kept his troops active in the lower Valley, foraging mainly, but occasionally making dashes into Winchester, the lower valley of the South Branch of the Potomac, and even as far as the vicinity of New Creek or toward Cumberland, sometimes breaking the Baltimore and Ohio Railroad but never very seriously. These forays compelled the strengthening of the Federal garrisons along the line of the railway, especially at Harper's Ferry, Martinsburg and New Creek. The garrison at Petersburg was withdrawn to New Creek January 31st, for the reason that its exposed position and distance from New Creek rendered it very difficult to maintain, especially in stormy weather, over the mountain roads. On the 29th of January, 1864, two brigades of Confederates under Early and Rosser, which had come over from the Shenandoah, captured an important wagon train near Medley, on the road from New Creek to Petersburg, dispersing the wagon guard and driving it back to New Creek. The following day the troops at Petersburg having discovered the presence of so strong a force of Confederates approaching from Moorefield, and being nearly out of provisions, fell back to New Creek by way of Greenland Gap, followed by the enemy, who, however, did not attack there, but turned off toward Burlington and Patterson's Creek to the railroad, where Rosser destroyed two bridges within eight miles of Cumberland, after capturing the guards, and then made good his escape by way of Sheet's Mill and Romney, up the South Branch of the Potomac, rejoining Early at Moorefield and eluding a force of Federal cavalry sent from Martinsburg to Wardensville and Romney to intercept the raiders. All the force from New Creek that could be spared moved out toward Moorefield via Purgittsville, where a junction was made with the mounted troops from Martinsburg, but too late to recover either the captured wagons or the prisoners, who, covered by their escort of infantry, cavalry and artillery, effected their escape up the South Fork Valley and thence over to Lost River and the Shenandoah via Brock's Gap. This was the last raid made by the Confederates in that direction until later in the year. Early claims they brought out, besides the 50 wagons and their teams, 1,200 cattle, 500 sheep and 78 prisoners.

Few of those who campaigned during the Civil War through these beautiful valleys, whether they wore the gray or the blue, were aware they were on historic ground, where Washington in his youth, first as a surveyor and then as a soldier, had already penetrated. The beetling crags that frown upon the radiant valley of the South Branch of the Potomac had seen George Washington first come into those undisturbed fastnesses a young lad of sixteen, with transit and surveyor's chain, to define for Lord Fairfax the western limits of his vast land grant.

Those same mountains saw Washington come there again in 1753, at the age of twenty-one, a major and adjutant-general of the Virginia militia, but sent by Governor Dinwiddie to warn off the French troops sent from Canada to establish themselves in the Ohio River Valley. Washington's errand took him through Winchester, then already a flourishing frontier town, to Will's Creek (now the City of Cumberland), where, with a few companions, he plunged farther into the wilderness northward toward Lake Erie, until he came to the fort, within fifteen miles of the lake, where was found the commanding officer of the French expedition, M. de St. Pierre, and to whom Washington delivered the Governor's notice, which De St. Pierre forwarded to the Governor of Canada, the Marquis Duquesne.

No attention being paid to Governor Dinwiddie's warning, and the intended encroachments of the French into what was claimed by the colonies as British crown lands, having become well defined, the colonies, under the lead of Virginia, prepared to dispute with the French and their savage Indian allies the possession of the Valley of the Ohio. Washington, as lieutenant-colonel, commanded a small force of four companies at Will's Creek, afterwards called Fort Cumberland, then the most exposed and advanced post on the frontier, confronted by a much stronger party of French, who had established themselves on the Ohio River, where Pittsburg stands now, but which was then called Fort Duquesne and afterwards Fort Pitt. This was in 1754.

At the age of twenty-three we find Washington again at Winchester as a volunteer *aide-de-camp* to General Braddock, who had been sent out from England with two regiments of regular troops to operate from Fort Cumberland against the French and Indians in the Ohio country. The disastrous march to Fort Duquesne soon followed and Braddock's defeat was the result. Braddock himself was mortally wounded and died four days after; his troops became panic-stricken and precipitately retreated to Fort Cumberland.

Virginia then provided a new army of sixteen companies and gave the command to Washington, who fixed his headquarters at Winchester, with advanced parties along the frontier from Fort Cumberland south to Fort Dinwiddie, on Jackson's River. This line must have extended up the South Branch Valley to its head, where Monterey now stands, and then down Jackson's River to Covington. Sparks, in his "Life of Washington," says "he performed a tour of inspection among the mountains, visiting all the outposts along the frontier." So all the country raided through by Averell in 1863 and defended by Sam. Jones, Imboden, W. L. Jackson, Echols, and others was more than a hundred years before patrolled by Washington and his hardy troopers. A large fort was built by Washington at Winchester in 1756 which was called Fort Loudoun in honor of the Earl of Loudoun, who had come out from England to command all the troops in the American colonies.

Fort Duquesne was abandoned by the French in November, 1758, and destroyed, the garrison escaping down the Ohio River in boats; a small force of two hundred Virginians was left there and the name changed to Fort Pitt. The remainder of the Virginia troops returned to Winchester. Washington resigned his commission in the Virginia militia the last week in December, 1758, when he was only twenty-six years of age, and settled down again at Mount Vernon until he was called to command the Continental Army, June 15, 1775.

CHAPTER IX, THE DUBLIN DEPOT, NEW MARKET AND LYNCHBURG CAMPAIGNS

On the 29th of February, 1864, a special order, by direction of the President, was issued assigning Maj.-Gen. Franz Sigel to the command of the Department of West Virginia, and that officer assumed command on the 10th of March, thus superseding Maj.-Gen. B. F. Kelley. The headquarters of the Department were located at Cumberland, Md.

On the 10th of March, also, Lieut-Gen. U. S. Grant was assigned by the President to the command of the armies of the United States, pursuant to an Act of Congress, approved February 29, 1864, by which Grant was made a Lieutenant-General. Major-General Halleck, at his own request, was relieved from duty as Commander-in-Chief of the Army, but was retained as Chief of Staff. General Meade was also retained in command of the Army of the Potomac, although General Grant, during the remainder of the war, made his headquarters with and personally directed the movements of that army.

From his headquarters at Cumberland, General Sigel at once proceeded to reorganize and partially redistribute his troops, preparatory to taking the field. He placed all his mounted troops belonging to the First and Fourth Divisions under General Averell, commanding the Fourth Division, which then became known as the Cavalry Division, at Martinsburg, and took away Averell's infantry, which he gave to Sullivan's Division at Harper's Ferry. He retained Mulligan's Division unchanged, at New Creek, and Moor's two regiments at Beverly.

About this period Early's Division of infantry and Rosser's Brigade of cavalry were withdrawn from the Valley and rejoined Lee at Gordonsville, leaving Imboden, together with Mosby's, White's and Gilmor's battalions (all rangers) to operate in the Shenandoah region.

General Grant, on assuming command of all the armies, proceeded first to reorganize and consolidate the Army of the Potomac into three army corps - (the Second, Fifth and Sixth, commanded respectively by Generals Hancock, Warren and Sedgwick), and made preparations for an early advance on Richmond from the line of the Rapidan. Among other collateral movements contemplated was an expedition from Beverly, W. Va., and one from the Kanawha, to break the Virginia and Tennessee Railroad in Southwestern Virginia. Of the first named he gave the command to Gen. E. O. C. Ord and the latter to Gen. George Crook. Although the troops composing both expeditions were to be taken from General Sigel's Department of-West Virginia, both Ord and Crook received their instructions direct from General Grant.

On the 29th of March Sigel reported the strength and location of the troops of the Department of West Virginia, as follows:

Infantry, 15,680; cavalry, 5,441; artillery, 2,276—divided into three infantry divisions and one of cavalry.

The Cavalry Division, under Averell, in front of Martinsburg, with a line of outposts from the Shenandoah River to Back Creek, sending out patrols for thirty miles south, southwest, and west.

The First Infantry Division (Sullivan's), occupying Harper's Ferry, Martinsburg, Frederick and the line of the railroad from Monocacy River to Sleepy Creek.

The Second Infantry Division (Mulligan's) scattered along the railroad from Sleepy Creek (near Hancock) to Parkersburg, with advanced posts at Philippi, Buckhannon, Bulltown, Glenville and Wirt Court-House. There were two regiments of infantry holding Beverly, under Colonel Moor, temporarily attached to Averell's Cavalry Division, but New Creek was the most important point on this line.

The remainder of Sigel's troops constituted a Third Division, under Crook, who occupied the Kanawha and Gauley River region, with an outpost at Fayette Court-House. Only a few of the above-mentioned positions were fortified with guns mounted.

On the same day that Sigel made the report of the location of the troops of his department, General Grant directed him to concentrate at Beverly and Charleston the troops to make up the two expeditions under Ord and Crook, those at Beverly to number not less than 8,000 infantry, three batteries and 1,500 cavalry. Crook, from Charleston on the Kanawha, was to move at the same time as Ord, throwing his infantry as far south as the passes in the mountains held by the Confederates, to prevent them coming north, and, with his cavalry, Crook was to force his way through to the Virginia and Tennessee Railroad, then move eastward to join Ord.

The Confederate commander of the region to be passed over by these expeditions was Maj.-Gen. John C. Breckinridge, who, by an order dated Richmond, February 25, 1864, had relieved Gen. Sam. Jones of what was known as the Trans-Allegheny, or Western Department of Virginia. It contained an aggregate of 7,000 troops present, organized into two brigades of infantry (Echols's and McCausland's) and W. L. Jackson's Brigade of cavalry, with seven batteries. Echols was stationed between Union and Lewisburg, and McCausland at the Narrows of New River. Their main base was at Dublin Depot, on the Virginia and Tennessee Railroad. Jackson's cavalry was in the vicinity of Warm Springs, Bath County, watching the approaches by way of the valleys of the South Branch of the Potomac and the Greenbrier.

By the middle of March all these troops were on the alert for any Federal raids, already reported by Confederate scouts as being in preparation; the passes through that difficult mountain region were not blockaded by fallen timber, were fortified, and arrangements made to organize and call out the "minute men" of the entire region bordering upon the eastern slope of the Allegheny Mountains, as far south as the Virginia and Tennessee Railroad.

These "minute men" were first provided for by an Act of the Confederate Congress approved April 16, 1862, known as the Public Defense Act, by which all men of the ages between eighteen and thirty-five were called to arms for three years, but where an excess of such men existed in any State over the number required to fill to a maximum the regiments already organized from that State, the surplus were to be held as reserves for any future calls from that State. By an Act, approved February 17, 1864, the age limit was made to include all white men between the ages of seventeen and fifty, those only being called to the ranks who were between eighteen and forty-five, and all others held as reserves or for local defense, or, as General Lee called them, "minute men."

In a letter to Gen. Braxton Bragg, who, on the 24th of February, 1864, was assigned to direct all the armies of the Confederate States, General Lee says (April 7): "I think it apparent that the enemy is making large preparations for the approaching campaign in Virginia. I think every preparation should be made to meet the approaching storm, which will apparently burst on Virginia, and unless its force can be diverted by an attack in the West, that troops should be collected to oppose it. With our present supplies on hand, the interruption of the trains on the Southern roads would cause the abandonment of Virginia."

Longstreet's Corps, which, after its bitter experience at Chickamauga and at Knoxville, had wintered at Morristown and Newmarket, in upper East Tennessee, was ordered on the 7th of April to rejoin Lee via Lynchburg. Ransom's Division was left in East Tennessee.

The Federal prisoners and all paroled Confederates were removed from Richmond, as well as much of the useless population, so as to diminish the number of mouths to feed and enable the accumulation of subsistence there for the combatants.

The preparations for an advance of all the Federal armies simultaneously were perfected by General Grant during the month of April, to take place early in May, and included a force of about 25,000 men, under Gen. B. F. Butler, from the direction of Norfolk and Fortress Monroe, who was to move on Richmond along the south side of the James River and establish a base on that river at City Point. This was accomplished on the 5th of May.

We have already seen the arrangement for the two expeditions, from Beverly and the Kanawha, to cut the Virginia and Tennessee Railroad in Southwestern Virginia, where the two commands were to join and then move northward toward the Army of the Potomac by way of Lynchburg.

General Grant himself, with the Army of the Potomac, greatly strengthened by the return of convalescents and furloughed men as well as by new troops, was to move directly upon General Lee's army and force it to accept battle or to retire upon Richmond.

To secure against any strengthening of Lee's army from other Confederate armies, especially from the direction of Georgia, General Sherman, with a powerful force of over 100,000 men, made up from troops from East Tennessee and Mississippi, with Thomas's splendid army at Chattanooga as a nucleus, was to move upon Gen. Joe Johnston's army at Dalton simultaneously with Grant's and Butler's movements upon Richmond, and "to get into the interior of the enemy's country as far as you can."

Still another factor in Grant's general scheme was a movement on Mobile by Banks's army from the direction of New Orleans, but this part of the plan had to be abandoned because of the delay in getting Banks's army back from his Red River expedition into Texas, which had proved such a dismal failure. The general project thus consisted originally of a grand left wheel simultaneously by all the armies in the field east of the Mississippi River, with the Army of the Potomac as a pivot, or, as General Grant in his letters to Sherman stated it, "to work all parts of the army together, and somewhat toward a common center."

All of the foregoing movements were to be made simultaneously on a telegraphic signal from Grant.

During April the weather was so stormy and the roads through the mountains of West Virginia were so unpromisingly bad, that General Grant, on General Sigel's advice, abandoned that part of his plan which related to the expedition under General Ord from Beverly southward via Covington to cut the Virginia and Tennessee Railroad, and General Ord, on the 19th of April, was relieved from the command at his own request, although the troops who were to compose the movements had already been concentrated at Grafton, Webster and Beverly, thus leaving the Baltimore and Ohio Railroad east of Cumberland very much depleted of its guarding forces.

As a substitute for the Ord expedition from Beverly, General Grant at the last moment authorized Sigel, at that general's suggestion, to organize a force of about 7,000 men for an aggressive movement up the Shenandoah Valley on Staunton and beyond, where he could be joined by Crook's column of 10,000 men from the Kanawha. Sigel's column was concentrated at Martinsburg by the 28th of April, and moved out toward Winchester and Strasburg on the 2d of May, Crook's expedition from Charleston, W. Va., starting the same day, one column through Logan Court-House toward Saltville and another through Fayette Court-House toward the Virginia and Tennessee Railroad.

The Sigel column, marching up the Shenandoah, soon came to grief. At the very outset Mosby, with his ranger battalion (known as the Forty-third Virginia Cavalry), harassed Sigel on his left flank and rear, at Bunker Hill, Martinsburg, Winchester and Front Royal, capturing wagons, animals and prisoners.

The partisans under Imboden and McNeill also took advantage of the weakening of the Federal garrisons along the railroad from New Creek westward to raid that section successfully early in May, and destroyed considerable railroad property at Piedmont, capturing the guards. Another and larger party on the 10th of May, under Imboden in person, attacked a small party of Federal cavalry from the direction of Lost River and Brock's Gap on the road leading from Wardensville to Moorefield, driving the Federals out toward Romney and Springfield. The Federal train was lost but most of the horses were saved. The Federal party, under Colonel Higgins, of the Twenty-second Pennsylvania Cavalry, lost also about fifty men killed, wounded and missing. Imboden then withdrew hastily to Mount Jackson, in the upper Shenandoah Valley, by way of Brock's Gap.

After some preliminary cavalry skirmishing at Rude's Hill and the town of New Market, Sigel engaged the enemy under Breckinridge, two miles south of the latter place, on the morning of the 15th of May, and was repulsed with the loss of five guns, about 600 killed and wounded and 50 prisoners. Sigel then safely retreated to Strasburg and behind Cedar Creek. His force in the action consisted of Moor's and Thoburn's Brigades of infantry, a brigade and a half of cavalry and five batteries of artillery, in all less than 6,000 men. Breckinridge's command consisted of Echols's and Wharton's infantry brigades (which had been hastily brought from near Union and the Narrows of New River, West Virginia, to Staunton), a battalion of cadets from the Lexington (Va.) Military Institute, Imboden's Brigade, White's and Gilmor's Battalions of mounted partisans, and several batteries of artillery, in all about 8,000 men. Except the partisans, these were all concentrated by Breckinridge at Staunton and marched from there down the Valley through Harrisonburg to meet Sigel's approach.

After his defeat at New Market, Sigel was superseded in command of the Shenandoah column by General David Hunter on the 21st of May, but Sigel was retained in command of the Reserve Division, holding the line of the Baltimore and Ohio Railroad from the Monocacy to Cumberland.

Hunter on taking command immediately resumed the march on Staunton through Harrisonburg and Port Republic, avoiding Breckinridge's forces at Mount Crawford on the direct route. Staunton was reached on the 6th of June after a very spirited engagement with the Confederates, about 6,000 strong, under command of W. E. Jones, at a small town called Piedmont, seven miles southwest of Port Republic. This battle lasted all day of the 5th of June, finally resulting in the complete defeat and dispersion of the Confederates, with a loss to them of about 600 killed and wounded (Gen. W. E. Jones being left dead upon the field), over 1,000 prisoners (including 60 officers), and a large number of fugitives. The remnant of the command, under Gen. J. C. Vaughn, then retreated on Waynesborough to the eastward through Fishersville. Hunter's losses did not exceed 500 in killed, wounded and missing.

The reason why Breckinridge was not in command of the Confederate troops at Piedmont was that he had been ordered by General Lee, on the 17th of May, to bring his command by rail from Staunton to Hanover Junction, after leaving a guard for the Valley. That guard consisted of Imboden's Brigade, 3,000 strong.

W. E. Jones' and Vaughn's Brigades, after Crook had turned north again from the line of the Virginia and Tennessee Railroad at Christiansburg, were ordered by General Lee to move by rail from their stations at Glade Spring and Dublin Depot, on the 30th of May, with all their available forces, to the assistance of Imboden in the Valley, against whom Hunter's column was then advancing. Jones, being the senior in rank, assumed the command of Vaughn's, Imboden's, and his own Brigades, in the absence of General Breckinridge with Echols's and Wharton's Brigades, which had reported to General Lee at Hanover Junction on the 21st of May and had afterwards participated in the Battles of Cold Harbor.

Staunton was occupied without opposition, as it had been entirely depleted of regular troops. Indeed, there was no Confederate force left in the Valley except Gilmor's and McNeill's small parties of partisans, who were operating near Winchester and Moorefield. At Staunton, Hunter paroled several hundred sick and wounded Confederates and destroyed much Confederate property and supplies, besides effectually crippling the Virginia Central Railroad,

Another Confederate force of two brigades (McCausland's and W. L. Jackson's), which had been operating against Crook on and near the Virginia and East Tennessee Railroad, but under orders to join Breckinridge at Staunton, had moved as far as Buffalo Gap, ten miles west of Staunton, to interpose between Crook and Hunter, to delay if not to prevent their columns joining, Crook being then marching on Staunton from Lewisburg. As soon as Hunter reached Staunton, McCausland moved southward toward Lexington and left the way clear for Crook's column to move into Staunton, unopposed, on the 8th of June, with his troops in fine condition. On his way eastward Crook had destroyed all the railroad bridges, depots, etc., from the western terminus at Covington onward.

The operations of Crook's Kanawha column, before its junction with Hunter, had been fraught with great results, but on account of exceptional difficulties had not accomplished all that had been laid out for it. It had found Saltville too strongly held by the Confederates to justify an attack on the saltworks, after a most difficult march through a sparsely settled mountain region and with the most refuse transportation the West Virginia Quartermaster's Department could contrive to furnish.

Crook left Charleston by the Lewisburg road on the 2d of May, detaching at Camp Piatt a picked mounted column of 2,500 men under Averell to proceed to Saltville via Logan and Wyoming Court-Houses, Abb's Valley and Jeffersonville, then to move eastward along the Virginia and Tennessee River to rejoin Crook. This latter, with the main body of his troops, numbering 6,155 infantry, moved parallel with Averell on a road farther east, to the southward through Fayette Court-House and over Flat Top Mountain to Princeton, finding on his arrival there a small party of Confederate cavalry which was readily dispersed in the direction of Rocky Mount. McCausland's Confederate Infantry Brigade had left Princeton the day before Crook's arrival, leaving their camps standing, apparently not expecting any enemy to come upon Princeton, and had marched toward Dublin to take cars for Lynchburg and Staunton to reinforce Breckinridge against Sigel in the Shenandoah. McCausland reached Dublin on the 7th of May, where he was held by Gen. A. G. Jenkins, commanding that region in the absence of General Breckinridge, and marched back five miles on the 8th to Cloyd's Farm, to meet Crook, who was approaching from Princeton. Here Jenkins took up a strong position with McCausland's Brigade and gave battle to Crook on the 9th on Walker's Mountain, which resulted in a disastrous defeat to the Confederates and their precipitate retreat to and through Dublin to Salem. General Jenkins was among the wounded and the command then devolved upon McCausland, who was reinforced at Dublin by 500 men from John H. Morgan's command from Saltville.

At Cloyd's the Confederate losses were several hundred killed and wounded and 230 prisoners, while Crook's was 27 killed, 117 wounded, and 25 missing. It may be here noted that during the last two years of the Civil War the Confederate reports never showed either the strength of their troops in action or their casualties.

Crook captured and destroyed many valuable public stores and then moved out to New River Railroad Bridge on the 10th of May, where he found McCausland's troops drawn up on the east side. These he dispersed with his artillery and then destroyed the important railroad bridge which had been the unattainable object of several Federal expeditions during the preceding three years.

Crook says that at Dublin he found dispatches from Richmond stating that General Grant had been defeated, which determined him to move to Lewisburg as soon as possible. On the 10th of May Grant was attacking Lee at Spottsylvania, and these dispatches may have been concocted to encourage those Confederates away from Richmond who had commenced to despair of success. It is certain that Lee could not detach any part of his troops in the Wilderness, at Spottsylvania or Cold Harbor, and until after Grant had crossed to the south side of James River, to go to the assistance of his sorely-pressed troops in the Shenandoah Valley or in Western Virginia. His losses had been enormous (John Tyler said 18,000), but not so great as Grant's, who, between May 4 and June 15, had lost in killed, wounded and missing 52,789 officers and men; but these could be replaced by fresh levies at the North, whereas Lee's losses in men could not be restored, for the Confederacy had then exhausted its available fighting strength.

From New River, Crook commenced to put into execution his determination to return to Lewisburg, so he crossed New River below or north of the destroyed railroad bridge, at Pepper's Ferry, and marched to Blacksburg, thence to Union and, via Alderson's Ferry of the Greenbrier, to Meadow Bluff. He was joined at Union by Averell on the 15th of May.

Averell, after an exceedingly difficult march through the mountains, had come out at Jeffersonville on his way to Saltville, when he learned that place was held in strength by W. E. Jones's (who was shortly afterward killed near Staunton) and John H. Morgan's commands, so Averell turned toward Wytheville, where the lead works are located. On the 10th of May he engaged the enemy there, finding him to consist of part of the Saltville garrison, which had been hurriedly sent to its defense, and was also under orders to join Breckinridge at Staunton by way of Lynchburg. This was occurring while Crook, on a road farther east, was pursuing the remnants of McCausland's and A. G. Jenkins's Brigades through Dublin and at New River Railroad Bridge.

At Wytheville the enemy gave Averell considerable resistance and caused him a loss of 114 officers and men killed and wounded; besides Averell did not succeed in destroying the lead works. The Confederates retired from Wytheville during the night of the 10th and Averell moved to Dublin on the 11th, crossed New River on the 12th, followed by Morgan and Jones as far as the river, which they could not cross. Averell then moved to Christiansburg, and thence followed Crook's route over the mountains to Union, where he overtook Crook on the 15th.

While the foregoing operations up the Shenandoah and from the Kanawha were progressing, General Grant, with the Army of the Potomac, had crossed the Rapidan at Germanna and Ely's Fords, on the 4th of May, and was attacking Lee's army at the Wilderness, Spottsylvania Court-House and Cold Harbor. Grant's largely superior strength prevented Lee from detaching any of his troops to the assistance of his depleted West Virginia and Shenandoah forces, as he was fully occupied in holding his own against Grant's murderous assaults or his dangerous flanking movements.

With the accession of Crook's forces at Staunton, Hunter had a command of over 15,000 men, with thirty guns, but both he and Crook were a long distance from any base either on the Potomac or on the Kanawha, being entirely dependent upon their wagon trains for supplies, and especially for ammunition. Crook, however, had established a secondary base at Meadow Bluff, which, in turn, was dependent on Charleston, W. Va.

Behind both columns, particularly through the Shenandoah Valley back to the Baltimore and Ohio Railroad, the inhabitants were thoroughly hostile and the country swarming with guerillas, partisans and home-guards, through which supply trains could not penetrate without a small army to guard them. Mosby was especially active in the region about Strasburg, along Hunter's line of communication back to Harper's Ferry, his true base, so, after passing Harrisonburg, Hunter abandoned that route altogether for replenishing his stores.

At Staunton, Hunter disembarrassed himself of his empty and surplus wagons and the prisoners taken at Piedmont, by sending them to Beverly, by way of Buffalo Gap and west of the Alleghenies, under escort of Colonel Moor and 800 men, whose terms of enlistment had expired. This he could do with comparative safety, as the country west and northwest of Staunton had been cleared temporarily of any large force of Confederates.

On the 10th of June, with his own column and Crook's, Hunter resumed his movement on Lexington and Lynchburg, opposed at first only by a small force of Confederate cavalry — 2,000 men and a battery — under McCausland, which was easily driven into and through Lexington on the 11th, although the remnants of Vaughn's command, 2,500 strong, still remained on Hunter's left and rear at Waynesborough and Rockfish Gap, but too much disorganized since the Battle of Piedmont to be seriously considered.

The character of the country south of Staunton and beyond Lexington to the East Tennessee and Virginia Railroad is a continuation of the beautiful Valley of Virginia, bounded on the east by the softly-lined Blue Ridge and on the west by the outer ridges of the Alleghenies.

In the reorganization of his army at Staunton, Hunter gave the command of the Cavalry Division, which had accompanied his column from Cedar Creek, to Alfred Napoléon Alexander Duffié (1833 –1880) a French-American soldier. Duffié relieved Stahel, who had been wounded and sent back with the train to Beverly. Part of Stahel's mission was to get a re-supply of ammunition for Hunter's column, which, however, it was found impracticable to forward to him.

Early on the 10th of June, Duffié's cavalry was sent out on the Waynesborough turnpike to make a demonstration on Vaughn's command, then to turn south to Tye River Gap. Imboden's and W. L. Jackson's Confederate Cavalry Brigades moved north and east of Duffié's column. Near the Gap, Duffié destroyed Mount Torry Furnace, where Confederate pig-iron was being made; the Gap was passed by an almost impassable mountain road to the head of Tye River on the 11th, and thence Duffié marched on Amherst, near which place a courier from Hunter overtook him on the 12th with orders to rejoin Hunter at Lexington. Imboden, by passing through Howardsville Gap and east of the Southwest Mountains, succeeded in reaching Lynchburg on the 14th, which, up to that time, had barely 1,200 men under General Nicholls to defend it. So, had Duffié not been recalled, he might easily have entered Lynchburg two days before Imboden got there. Instead, Duffié rejoined Hunter at Lexington by way of White's Gap on the 13th.

On the second day out from Staunton, June 11th, Duffié had come up with, in Tye River Valley, and destroyed for the most part, a valuable wagon train of Confederate stores, specie, bonds, records and money, capturing with it about 40 prisoners, 7 of whom were officers. This train had been hurriedly sent away from Staunton toward Lynchburg on Hunter's approach to the former place after the Battle of Piedmont. That same afternoon Duffié sent a small party to the Virginia and Tennessee Railroad at Arrington Depot, where they burned the depot and several small bridges, and tore up the track, besides destroying a large quantity of boots, shoes and other Confederate quartermaster stores.

On the 12th, when near White's Gap, a small refugee wagon train loaded with provisions and forage was captured, and on the morning of the 13th, not far from Lexington, Duffié destroyed about 2,000 cords of wood, which had been cut to manufacture into charcoal. Another furnace for making pig-iron was also burned.

Hunter was in Lexington from the 11th to the 14th of June. While there he destroyed a great quantity of

Confederate and State property, including the Virginia Military Institute and the residence of Governor John Letcher. He also captured a few prisoners and eleven pieces of artillery; the latter were destroyed.

On the 13th Hunter sent Averell's Cavalry Division forward to Buchanan, on the James River, and on the 14th followed with his entire command. Before leaving Lexington, Hunter learned of the large force under Early that General Lee had detached to the succor of Lynchburg, but as that place was still feebly held, Hunter pushed on. At Buchanan he found that Averell had driven McCausland across the James, but not before McCausland had destroyed the bridge; a practicable ford was, however, found nearby. At Buchanan a number of barges in the James River Canal, loaded with stores, fell into Hunter's hands, and such as were not needed by his command were destroyed.

On the 15th Hunter moved by the Peaks of Otter road to Liberty, on the Virginia and Tennessee Railroad, twenty-four miles from Lynchburg. At Liberty a picked party of 200 cavalrymen, which Averell had sent out from Lexington to ride around Lynchburg, reported. They had crossed the Blue Ridge and struck the Charlottesville Railroad near Amherst, tearing up considerable track. Thence they had moved southeastward and crossed the James eight miles below Lynchburg, destroying two railroad trains and the depot on the South Side Railroad at Concordia; thence, passing through Campbell Court House, they moved south of Lynchburg to Liberty. They met with trifling loss.

On the 16th the movement on Lynchburg was resumed from Liberty. Duffié's cavalry was sent to the left on the Forestville road, sending out a strong reconnaissance toward Balcony Falls. Crook's Infantry Division followed the railroad, destroying it as they advanced. Averell's cavalry and Sullivan's Division of Infantry, with the reserve artillery and the train, moved on the Bedford turnpike. Averell crowded back McCausland, but in the afternoon found that he had been reinforced and was becoming stubborn. That night (the 16th) Hunter encamped seven miles east of Liberty, with his cavalry thrown out to the Great Otter River. Here General Hunter divested himself of an empty supply train of 200 wagons and sent it, under guard of an Ohio regiment, by way of New Castle, Sweet Springs and Lewisburg to Charleston, W. Va.

Late in the afternoon of the 11th the enemy was found strongly posted at Diamond Hill, on the Bedford road, five miles from Lynchburg, from which point he was driven into the town by Crook's infantry, killing and wounding a number of Confederates and capturing 70 prisoners and one gun. It was then unmistakably ascertained that Breckinridge had reached Lynchburg from Waynesborough with all his troops, but it being too late in the day for further operations, Hunter camped for the night on the battlefield. He was still ignorant of the near approach of Early's Corps (late Ewell's), which commenced to arrive via Charlottesville from Richmond the afternoon of the 17th, but that also was developed early on the morning of the 18th of June, when Hunter pushed forward his skirmishers to the toll-gate, two miles from the town, and a brisk fire was opened from the Confederate works, which was kept up throughout the forenoon. In this position Hunter was finally assaulted by the Confederates, who were repulsed and driven back into their main redoubts with considerable loss.

Hunter says: "It had now become sufficiently evident that the enemy had concentrated a force of at least double the numerical strength of mine, and what added to the gravity of the situation was the fact that my troops had scarcely enough of ammunition left to sustain another well-contested battle. I immediately ordered all the baggage and supply trains to retire by the Bedford turnpike and made preparations to withdraw the army as soon as it became sufficiently dark to conceal the movement from the enemy."

It being impossible for Hunter to return to the Shenandoah by way of Lexington and Staunton, he retired westward through Liberty and Buford's Gap during the 19th, 20th, and 21st, to Salem, "destroying all the bridges, depot buildings and contents on the railroad," being unmolested except by an occasional rear-guard action between his own and the Confederate cavalry. The most serious of these affairs occurred near Salem early on the 21st, when he suffered the loss of two batteries moving on the New Castle road, which, being insufficiently guarded, were disabled and spiked by the Confederate cavalry and the horses carried off. The guns, however, were recovered by Hunter's cavalry, and the Confederates in turn driven away with loss, but eight of the pieces had to be abandoned finally, after destroying all their carriages, for the lack of horses to haul them. After passing Catawba Valley, on the New Castle road, the pursuit ended, and Hunter moved on leisurely to Meadow Bluff, where he arrived on the 25th, and found ample supplies.

Hunter's losses in this campaign foot up 103 killed, 564 wounded and 271 missing, from June 10 to 23. He was so far beyond possible support, or even communication by courier, that dispatches could not reach him after he had passed south of Staunton. General Grant endeavored to send two divisions of Sheridan's cavalry to Hunter's assistance by way of Charlottesville, expecting Hunter to be in that vicinity, but Sheridan was attacked by Wade Hampton's and Fitzhugh Lee's cavalry at Trevilian Station of the Virginia Central Railroad on the 11th of June, and compelled to withdraw to the White House, on the Pamunkey, over the circuitous route north of the North Anna by which he had come. Although Sheridan had started from Grant's army on the 7th of June, Breckinridge's two brigades succeeded in passing from Lee's army over the railroad to Charlottesville and Waynesborough, before Sheridan could intercept them at Trevilian. Wade Hampton also had got into position so as to cover Gordonsville before Sheridan appeared at Trevilian and Fitzhugh Lee's Division had reached Louisa Court-House, only six miles from Trevilian.

While General Grant remained confronting General Lee at Cold Harbor it had been unsafe for the latter to detach more than Breckinridge's two small brigades to go to the relief of either Waynesborough or Lynchburg, but as soon as General Lee discovered, on the 12th, that General Grant had withdrawn from his front to cross to the south side of the James to join Butler, he, on the 13th, detached Early's entire Army Corps (formerly Ewell's) in hot haste to the relief of Lynchburg, which Early, with part of his troops, reached on the 17th, just in time to save the city from Hunter.

CHAPTER X

The Early Raid to Washington and the Return to the Valley

When Hunter placed his army south of Lynchburg and then withdrew to the Kanawha, he left the Valley and Washington uncovered except by the Federal troops on the line of the Baltimore and Ohio Railroad from Cumberland to the Monocacy, commanded by Sigel.

Early telegraphed General Lee from near Salem, on the 22d of June, that Hunter had made good his retreat into the West Virginia Mountains and that he (Early) would proceed the next day to carry out General Lee's original instructions. These were to move down into the Shenandoah Valley and into Maryland if practicable. In a letter to President Davis, June 29th, relating to Early's movements, General Lee says: "I still think it is our policy to draw the attention of the enemy to his own territory. It may force Grant to attack me, or weaken his forces. It will also, I think, oblige Hunter to cross the Potomac or expose himself to attack. From either of these events I anticipate good results. There will be time to shape Early's course, or terminate it, when he reaches the Potomac, as circumstances require. He could not be withdrawn from the Valley without inviting a return of Hunter's expedition. To retain him there inactive would not be disadvantageous. As before stated, my greatest present anxiety is to secure regular and constant supplies."

Part of General Lee's plans for Early contemplated the release of the Confederate prisoners at Point Lookout, Md.

It seems pertinent here to mention the great difficulty to obtain, and the high prices paid for, supplies at this period by the Confederate authorities. Besides the tithe required from all producers, there was an impressment law passed by the Confederate Congress, March 26, 1863, and subsequently amended, which was regulated by a tariff of prices to be paid for supplies taken, which tariff was established every two months by a Board of Appraisers in each State of the Confederacy, one member being appointed by the President and the other by the Governor of the State. For instance, the tariff for stores impressed in Virginia during October and November, 1864, gave the prices for wheat at $7.50 per bushel, flour from $33 to $42 per barrel, corn $5 per bushel, bacon $2.75 per pound, butter $5 per pound, horses and mules $800 per head, wood $8 per cord, potatoes $4 per bushel, onions $8 per bushel, New Orleans molasses $25 per gallon, Rio coffee $3 per pound, beef cattle $30 per 100 pounds, sheep $35 per head, pig-iron $278 to $350 per ton, cotton sheetings $1.75 per yard, army shoes $15 per pair, men's socks $2 per pair, apple and peach brandy $10 per gallon. All these prices were largely increased as the Confederate currency became further depreciated, so that in March, 1865, the last schedule furnished by the Virginia appraisers before they adjourned to May 2, 1865, showed the market price of wheat to be $25 per bushel, flour $126 per barrel, potatoes $20 per bushel, beef cattle $50 per hundred pounds, sheep $70 per head, army shoes $25 per pair, labor $8 per day. These were the prevailing market rates.

The suffering of the people and the difficulties of the Confederate Government became so great that in March, 1865, just before the close of the horrible drama, the Confederate Congress passed "An Act to raise coin for the purpose of furnishing necessary supplies for the Army," by which the Secretary of the Treasury was authorized to pledge cotton and tobacco for coin, not to exceed three millions of dollars, as a loan payable two years after ratification of a treaty of peace. The cotton and tobacco belonging to the Confederacy so pledged, was to be given safe conduct beyond the limits of the Confederacy "free from any molestation" to the exporter, or the payment of any duty. The attention of the officers of the army was called to the clause allowing the free exportation of the above-mentioned staples, and they were cautioned not to resist its operations. Cotton at Liverpool was then selling at $250 per bale of 400 pounds. Up to the passage of this Act no cotton was allowed to pass the Confederate lines into those of the United States.

Officers of the Confederate supply departments were calling upon Richmond for coin to enable them to obtain supplies even by impressment, as the holders of grain or provisions, especially in counties bordering upon the Potomac, refused the depreciated Confederate currency and demanded coin or "greenbacks."

Early had abandoned further pursuit of Hunter at Salem and turned his army northward through Buchanan and Fincastle in two columns, which passed through Lexington and Jackson's River Depot, converging at Staunton, and arriving there between the 25th and 27th of June. General Lee expected Hunter to refit and reorganize at Lewisburg and then return to the Valley, for, in a letter dated June 26 to President Davis, he says of Early: " I think it better that he should move down the Valley, if he can obtain provisions, which] would draw Hunter after him. If circumstances favor, I should also recommend his crossing the Potomac. I think I can maintain our lines here against General Grant. He does not seem disposed to attack and has thrown himself strictly on the defensive. I am less uneasy about holding our position than about our ability to procure supplies for the army. I fear the latter difficulty will oblige me to attack General Grant in his intrenchments, which I should not hesitate to do but for the loss it will inevitably entail."

At Staunton, Early rearranged his command, so that General Ransom, commanding all the cavalry in the Valley District, was relieved from duty with General Breckinridge and took his orders thereafter from Early direct. This cavalry command consisted of Col. Bradley T. Johnson's Brigade (formerly W. E. Jones's), to which Bradley Johnson's Mounted Maryland Battalion was added; Imboden's and W. L. Jackson's Brigades (formerly partisans, but now incorporated in the regular cavalry), and McCausland's Brigade (formerly A. G. Jenkins's).

Breckinridge's infantry was reorganized into two divisions, commanded respectively by himself and Maj.-Gen. J. B. Gordon.

The transportation for baggage was materially reduced.

On the 30th of June, Gen. Early passed beyond New Market northward, finding ample supplies of wheat and grass along his route. He detached Imboden to proceed down the South Branch Valley to the Baltimore and Ohio Railroad. Early camped near Winchester on the 2d of July, and, dividing his force, sent one column under Breckinridge to Martinsburg on the 3d, and with his own corps occupied Harper's Ferry on the 4th, the weak force of Federals retiring before both columns; those at Martinsburg, where Sigel had his headquarters, falling back to Shepherdstown, and the Harper's Ferry garrison to Maryland Heights. McCausland's Cavalry Brigade moved on the left of Breckinridge from Winchester via White Hall and down Back Creek, while the main cavalry under Ransom preceded Early's column of infantry on the 3d to Kearneysville via Brucetown and Leetown, having quite a lively engagement with the Federal cavalry at Kearneysville.

Early on the 4th, after McCausland's[xv] Mounted Brigade had captured the blockhouse at North Mountain Depot (Hedgesville), and destroyed the railroad, it swung around to Hainesville. Breckinridge's two divisions also broke the railroad east and west from Martinsburg, while the men of Early's Corps were similarly engaged from Harper's Ferry westward.

In the presence of such a very large body of Confederates (four divisions of infantry and one of cavalry) it was remarkable that Sigel should have been able to retire the small garrisons of Martinsburg and Harper's Ferry to the north side of the Potomac in safety and with so little loss of stores, but on the morning of the 5th of July he was able to report from Maryland Heights, where he had gone via Shepherdstown, that his own and Weber's commands were there and had provisions for twenty days, besides a liberal supply of ammunition. Weber partially destroyed the railroad bridge at Harper's Ferry after crossing, and took up the pontoons. Sigel intimated that he had no intention of abandoning the position, although he soon learned that Breckinridge had crossed that day to Sharpsburg and was foraging as far east as Boonsborough. Sigel reported his own force on Maryland Heights to be 6 regiments of infantry, 2,500 dismounted cavalry, 2 battalions of heavy artillery and 26 field guns. Nearby, in Pleasant Valley, there were about 1,000 mounted cavalry, 2 companies of artillery acting as infantry, and one 4 gun battery.

General Sigel was relieved by Gen. A. P. Howe on the 8th of July, the day the enemy disappeared from Harper's Ferry, after having sent Breckinridge's two infantry divisions the day before to feel the Federal position on Maryland Heights from the direction of Sharpsburg, but who found it too strong to assault.

Early then moved his entire force to the north side of the Potomac west of Harper's Ferry, and sending his cavalry, part to Frederick and part to Hagerstown, where it met some parties of Federal cavalry on observation, he moved his infantry column through Rohrersville, Boonsborough and Middletown to Frederick and Jefferson, Md., and thence, on the 9th, to the Monocacy River, where they met resistance which lasted throughout the day of the 9th, from troops hastily gathered at Baltimore by Gen. Lew Wallace and marched out to the Monocacy, to reinforce a small party under General Tyler already there. The object was to delay Early's progress toward Baltimore or Washington, at the iron railroad bridge and where the turnpikes to both Baltimore and Washington converge within a distance of two miles.

Wallace had thus succeeded in collecting a rather incongruous party of 2,500 men of all arms on the 6th of July, the Confederate cavalry being then only at Middletown. At this juncture Ricketts's Division of the Sixth Army Corps, which had been started from City Point by General Grant on the 7th of July on transports, commenced to arrive, and by daylight of the 9th two brigades (Truex's and McClennan's) 3,350 strong, were in position near Monocacy Bridge, thus increasing Wallace's command to nearly 6,000 men, but still a very weak force to oppose Early's vastly superior numbers. Wallace had but one field battery of six guns and one 24-pounder, as against at least 16 of Early's. Yet from 9 A. M. until 4 P. M. Wallace held his position, repulsing two infantry attacks, when, being heavily outflanked on his left, he threw all his force over to the other flank at the stone bridge on the Baltimore turnpike to cover the retreat to Baltimore. The bridge was held by General Tyler with his handful of men until after all the other troops had passed to his rear and he was virtually surrounded by Rodes's Division, when he cut his way through with the larger part of his troops. Wallace's losses were 1,294 killed, wounded and missing, mostly in Ricketts's Division; that of the Confederates is given by Early as 600 or 700, yet he left 435 of his wounded at Frederick, who could not bear transportation.

The great importance of the Battle of the Monocacy lay in the delay it caused Early in his march on Washington, thereby enabling the remainder of the Sixth Corps to reach the Capital from Grant's army, as well as the Nineteenth Army Corps from New Orleans, before Early could reach there, which he would have accomplished had he not been forced to march around Harper's Ferry and then been checked by Wallace at the Monocacy. These most important events saved the Capital from capture, and General Grant so accords it in both his official report and in his "Memoirs," notwithstanding which Sigel was relieved by Howe on the

8th of July and Wallace was superseded by Ord on the 11th, after he had marched his command safely back to Baltimore.

Sigel and Wallace between them had delayed Early's progress at least three days. The inscription Wallace proposed to place on the monument over his dead at the Monocacy— "These Men Died to Save the National Capital"—would not be amiss.

Making no pursuit of Wallace toward Baltimore, Early, on the day after the Battle of the Monocacy, resumed his march on Washington, through Rockville, where he turned to the left so as to get upon the Seventh street road. He appeared before Fort Stevens (now Brightwood) during the afternoon of the 11th of July and pushed his skirmishers up to within 40 rods of the defenses, driving in the small force of Veteran Reserves, convalescents from the hospitals, quartermasters' employees, and civilian volunteers gathered there to dispute his advance; but he made no general assault, giving as a reason that he found the works too strong and his men too much worn by the heat and the forced marching of the past two days. Then came the dramatic arrival of the two Divisions of Wright's Sixth Army Corps from City Point by water and the head of the Nineteenth Army Corps from New Orleans by ocean steamers, with Mr. Lincoln meeting them at the wharf and then going out to Fort Stevens to see in person what was being accomplished. It is said that as the President stood by the side of General Wright on the parapet of Fort Stevens, watching the movements of the skirmishing then in progress between Wheaton's Division of the Sixth Corps and the Confederates, as Wheaton was recovering the ground lost before his troops arrived on the line, an officer standing near the President was struck, and it was only this that induced the President to yield to the entreaties of those about him to no longer expose himself.

Early remained in close proximity to Fort Stevens throughout the 12th until night, skirmishing continually. His headquarters were at Silver Spring, about two miles north of Washington, at the house of Montgomery Blair, then Postmaster-General of the United States, which was destroyed when his army retreated, although Breckinridge pleaded with Early to save it. In passing through Hagerstown, Early had levied a contribution of $220,000 on the inhabitants and another of $200,000 at Frederick.

While Early was feeling the lines at Fort Stevens on the Seventh Street road, his cavalry, under McCausland, was demonstrating on the Georgetown road at Tenallytown and in front of Fort Reno. Mosby's Battalion of partisans was threatening to cross the Potomac at the Chain Bridge and move toward Georgetown by the River road. Both these points, however, were well protected.

When Early retired from in front of Washington during the night of the 12th, he moved through Rockville and thence crossed the Potomac to Leesburg, by way of Darnestown, Poolesville and White's Ford. He remained near Leesburg during the 14th and 15th.

At Frederick, on the 8th of July, Early had detached Bradley Johnson's cavalry to make a raid on the Northern Central and the Philadelphia and Baltimore railroads, which resulted in their being closed to traffic by the destruction of several bridges. The most notable was the burning of the bridge two miles long over Gunpowder Creek, 15 miles northeast of Baltimore, and the capture there of two passenger trains by Major Harry Gilmor, commanding a Mounted Maryland Battalion, which Gen. Bradley Johnson detached for that purpose. Part of the latter's mission was to endeavor to surprise the small garrison at Point Lookout, Md., where the Potomac enters Chesapeake Bay, and release the Confederate prisoners confined there; but from this he was recalled at Bladensburg by Early, when the latter had decided to withdraw south of the Potomac from in front of Washington.

While Early was ravaging Maryland and threatening the seat of the Federal Government, Hunter, with all the troops he had carried to the Kanawha from Lynchburg, was returning to the Valley as rapidly as he could, by boat up the Ohio to Parkersburg and thence eastward by rail. His advance left Charleston, on the Kanawha, on the 3d of July (the day Breckinridge occupied Martinsburg and Early reached the vicinity of Harper's Ferry) and his head of column reached Cumberland on the 9th (the day of the Battle of the Monocacy). Martinsburg was re-occupied by Hunter's cavalry on the 10th, followed soon after by Sullivan's Division, the first infantry to arrive from the West. (Early was then—July 14th—at Leesburg, and who, in a letter to General Lee, announced his intention to "start for the Valley in the morning. I will retreat in forced marches by land toward Richmond. "

Later events changed Early's intentions after he reached the Valley and had placed the Blue Ridge between his army and the pursuing column under Wright with the Sixth and part of the Nineteenth Army Corps. Wright was given command, by order of the President, July 13, 4.35 P. M., "of all the forces moving from Washington or elsewhere against the enemy," including any that might join him from the commands of Hunter, Ord, "or elsewhere."

For a while some difficulty was found in locating Hunter, owing to the breaks caused by the Confederates in both the railroad and the telegraph lines, although it was known that he had passed eastward through Cumberland toward Harper's Ferry. Finally he was reached at the latter place on the 15th by a special messenger, bearing instructions from General Grant, for Hunter to move with all his forces that had arrived from the west, and with Howe's troops at Maryland Heights, and then to form a junction with Wright's column to attack Early. Sullivan's Division and some detachments of Hunter's command, 8,000 strong, which had only then reached Harper's Ferry, immediately pushed out toward Hillsborough and Purcellville east of the Blue Ridge, preceded by the

Duffié cavalry, who struck into the rear of Early's column near Purcellville, and captured from it about 80 wagons and 50 prisoners, the main force of Confederates having passed about two hours before, headed for Snicker's Gap, in which direction Duffié , supported by Crook's troops, followed on the 17th, passing through the Gap and into the Valley, where the enemy was found drawn up in strength at the west side of the crossing of the Shenandoah River on the Berryville road. During the 18th Early remained in this position and resisted Crook's efforts to force a crossing, those troops which had succeeded in getting across farther downstream being forced to retire again to the east bank, with considerable loss. Ricketts's Division of the Sixth Corps, which had rejoined Wright from Baltimore, came up in time to cover Crook's retirement. The Confederate losses are not stated, but were also considerable.

Wright, with the Sixth Corps and two Divisions of the Nineteenth, as soon as Hunter's column under Crook had been located at Hillsboro, feeling uneasy about Crook's proximity to so largely a superior force of the enemy unsupported, crossed the Potomac at White's Ford, and followed the track of Early's army through Leesburg out on the Snicker's Gap road until he was joined by the head of Crook's column at Purcellville, when he sent him in advance to pursue Early into Snicker's Gap.

Another attempt was made to cross the Shenandoah early on the 20th, when it was found Early had retreated the night before, and had gone with his main army toward Front Royal and Strasburg, covering his trains. Early had thus succeeded in getting away with all his Maryland plunder, including several thousand head of horses, mules and cattle.

Wright then deemed the time had come to obey Grant's orders, communicated through Halleck, to return to Washington with the Sixth and Nineteenth Army Corps, preparatory to rejoining Grant at City Point, as Grant said, "before the enemy can get Early back;" for Grant then believed Early to be in full retreat on Richmond by way of the Valley. His dispatch of July 16th, 4.40 p. M., to Halleck, indicates that he expected Hunter's troops to be able, without any assistance from Wright, to pursue Early to Gordonsville and Charlottesville, break up the railroad there, etc. Grant adds: "I do not think there is now any further danger of an attempt to invade Maryland. The position of the enemy in the West and here (meaning Richmond) is such as to demand all the force they can get together to save vital points to them. As soon as the rebel army is known to have passed Hunter's forces, recall Wright and send him back here with all dispatch, and also send the Nineteenth Corps. If the enemy have any notion of returning, the fact will be developed before Wright can start back."

When Wright started to march back to Leesburg and Washington, Crook set out for Winchester by way of Berryville. He reached Winchester on the 22d, finding Averell and his Cavalry Division, with some infantry as supports, already there since the 21st, when he had entered Winchester unopposed, after quite a spirited affair on the afternoon of the 20th at Stephenson's Depot, north of Winchester, with Imboden's and Jackson's cavalry, supported by Ramseur's Division of Early's infantry, where Averell captured 4 guns, 17 officers and 250 men, killed 73 and wounded 130 of the enemy; his own loss being 53 killed, 155 wounded and 6 missing. Averell's Division was the last of Hunter's command to return from the Kanawha, so that on the 22d virtually all of that force was again reunited at Winchester, and was about 11,000 strong. Early's strength was estimated at 25,000.

The departure of Wright's two Army Corps for Washington was known in Richmond and by Early almost as soon as they started. Early's intention to "retreat in forced marches by land on Richmond" underwent a sudden change at Strasburg, for he turned back toward Winchester on the 22d and badly defeated Crook's command at Kernstown on the 23d, driving it through Winchester on the 24th and into Martinsburg on the 25th, where a stand was made during the day, and a retreat on Williamsport across the Potomac during the night was unopposed by Early, who followed only with his cavalry to the river. Crook then marched his infantry north of the river to Harper's Ferry, leaving his cavalry along the Potomac from Hancock to Harper's Ferry to guard the crossings. As Hunter had remained at Harper's Ferry while Crook commanded in the field, Hunter now resumed charge of all the troops within his Department. Crook's losses at Kernstown and during the retreat were 100 killed, 606 wounded and 579 missing. Early's losses were also severe.

Early then occupied Martinsburg, Smithfield and Bunker Hill with his infantry, his cavalry being thrown forward to the Potomac; his own headquarters were at Bunker Hill. The Valley was again in entire possession of the Confederates, and the Baltimore and Ohio Railroad, which had been placed in complete running order throughout its entire length on the 21st of July, was again interrupted as a means of Federal communication with the West.

As soon as Early had retired to the Valley from his raid on Washington, General Lee sent Fitzhugh Lee's Division of cavalry to Culpeper Court-House, to be used as a means of communication with Early and to gather fresh horses, its absentees, etc. These troops were found in position on the Rapidan on the 25th by a scouting party sent out from Washington. The trains on the Virginia Central Railroad were then running and bringing supplies from Richmond to Culpeper, which were there shipped by wagon trains to Early's command, via Front Royal. Eventually these troops, strengthened by Kershaw's Division of infantry under Gen. R. H. Anderson, joined Early in the Valley.

On the 21st of July, on representations made from Washington by Halleck, General Grant modified his orders about sending the Sixth Corps, and that part of the Nineteenth with Wright, to City Point. Grant's new instructions to Halleck read: "You may retain Wright's command until the departure of Early is assured, or other forces are collected to make its presence no longer necessary. I am now sending back all veterans whose terms of service expire previous to the 25th of August."

Wright's command all reached Washington by nightfall of the 23d (Early had then turned on Crook, and drove him through Winchester the next day). Grant at that time telegraphed Halleck as follows: "City Point, Va., July 23, 1864, 6 p. M.—If Wright has returned to Washington, send him immediately back here, retaining, however, the portion of the Nineteenth Corps now in Washington for further orders. Early is undoubtedly returning here to enable the enemy to detach troops to go to Georgia. That same morning Mr. Lincoln had telegraphed to General Hunter at Harper's Ferry: "Are you able to take care of the enemy when he turns back upon you, as he probably will do on finding out that Wright has left?" To which Hunter had immediately replied: "My force is not strong enough to hold the enemy should he return upon me with his whole force." And Early was then returning in full strength. At noon of the 24th General Grant telegraphed Halleck: "You can retain General Wright until I learn positively what has become of Early."

On the morning of the 26th of July Wright's column, about 19,000 strong, was again set in motion from Washington via Rockville for the Monocacy, to form a junction with Hunter's forces at such point as the latter might select. As already mentioned, Hunter's entire command, about 11,000 strong, was then at or near Harper's Ferry, with his cavalry (two Divisions) guarding the crossings of the Potomac on the north bank as far up as Hancock. In addition to authorizing the retention of Wright, General Grant dispatched from City Point all that portion of the Nineteenth Corps, which had been sent to the Army of the Potomac, when he learned that Baltimore and Washington were no longer seriously threatened. He also sent six more regiments of his cavalry. Of course, all these troops went by water. On the 30th General Grant sent Torbert's Division of Cavalry from the Army of the Potomac to Washington, followed on the 2d of August by General Sheridan in person, Grant's intention being then to give Sheridan command of all of Hunter's troops in the field; but, finding opposition existing to this arrangement at Washington, Grant deferred action until he could first confer with Hunter in person, which he soon after did.

Meanwhile, Wright's column had joined Hunter's at Harper's Ferry on the 29th of July, both commands, except Crook's cavalry, being assembled at Halltown, three miles south, on the Charlestown road. The next day the entire force was marched back toward Frederick to more effectually cover Baltimore and Washington. Kelley, at Cumberland, was strengthened by troops from Kentucky by way of Parkersburg.

Up to the 29th of July, besides an occasional demonstration by Confederate cavalry at the upper crossings of the Potomac, Early's troops were busily engaged foraging in the lower Valley and gathering the ripening crops; but on that date Early sent two of his mounted brigades, under McCausland and Bradley Johnson, to cross the Potomac at McCoy's Ferry and raid into Maryland and Pennsylvania. This force numbered about 2,600 men, commanded by McCausland, and moved via Clear Spring, Md., and Mercersburg to Chambersburg, Pa., where it appeared early on the 30th of July, brushing away to the eastward, all along the route, the feeble parties of Averell's Federal cavalry watching its progress from the direction of Hagerstown, where Averell had his headquarters. As soon as the enemy's strength and purpose had been developed, Averell gathered a considerable force of his cavalry and set out for Chambersburg via Greencastle, in pursuit, but did not reach there until some hours after McCausland had burned the town and fallen back toward McConnellsburg, westward.

McCausland on entering Chambersburg demanded a ransom of $100,000 in coin or $500,000 in United States currency, to be paid in three hours' time, failing which the town was fired in many places simultaneously, after a scene of most revolting villainies perpetrated by the Confederates. There exists no report from McCausland of events at Chambersburg, but Bradley Johnson recounts them in considerable detail.

McCausland, who had intended proceeding west from McConnellsburg toward Bedford, was so closely followed by Averell that he was forced to turn southward to Hancock. There, on the 31st, a ransom of $30,000 and 5,000 cooked rations were demanded under threat of destroying the town; but before they could be collected, McCausland was attacked by Averell, and hastily moved off with his command toward Cumberland, in front of which he appeared and engaged Kelley's troops late in the afternoon of August 1st. Finding Kelley too well prepared, McCausland drew off eastward after nightfall, abandoning his dead and wounded, and at Old Town forced a crossing of the Potomac at daylight of the 2d of August, capturing or dispersing a regiment of new troops from Ohio that Kelley had placed there to defend the crossing. The Confederates then moved south into the Valley of the South Branch of the Potomac, via Springfield and Romney.

From Romney, on the 4th of August, McCausland moved on New Creek (Keyser), and was repulsed in his attack on that fortified place, leaving 25 of his dead on the field when he moved off again that same day toward Moorefield, where he was surprised in camp by Averell on the morning of the 7th of August and routed, with a loss of 27 officers and 393 men prisoners, 4 guns and caissons complete, several hundred horses, equipments and small arms. The greater part of McCausland's forces were dispersed and retreated into the Shenandoah Valley through the mountain passes in small squads, which finally were assembled at Mount Jackson.

The movement later of Hunter's and Wright's combined commands from Harper's Ferry again to Frederick, except the strong force left behind under Howe to hold Maryland Heights, was the result of the commotion at the North and in Washington caused by the Chambersburg raid, together with hostile demonstrations along the line of the Potomac from Williamsport down to Leesburg. As soon as it was definitely ascertained that none of Early's infantry had crossed to the north side of the river, Hunter's infantry was marched to a line east of and along the Monocacy, to observe Early's movements in the lower Valley and be available to protect the Capital from any coup de main. It was in this position that Hunter was visited by General Grant on the 5th of August, which resulted in Hunter's asking to be relieved from command of the Department of West Virginia, and Sheridan, who had already reached Washington from City Point, being sent for to meet Grant at the Monocacy, when he was placed temporarily in command of the newly-formed Middle Military Division, comprised of the States of Maryland, Pennsylvania, West Virginia, the District of Columbia, and as much of Northern Virginia as was then occupied by the Federal army.

Grant had already ordered the troops assembled at the Monocacy to move back to Harper's Ferry and Halltown before Sheridan's arrival. The written instructions prepared for Hunter were given to Sheridan instead, and Grant returned to City Point.

CHAPTER XI
Sheridan's Campaigns—Battles of the Opequon, Fisher's Hill and Tom's Brook

The written instructions addressed to Hunter, which Sheridan received, were as follows:

"Monocacy Bridge, Md., "August s, 1864, 8 P. M. Maj.-Gen. D. Hunter:

"General—Concentrate all your available force without delay in the vicinity of Harper's Ferry, leaving only such railroad guards and garrisons for public property as may be necessary. Use, in this concentration, the railroad, if by so doing time can be saved. From Harper's Ferry, if it is found that the enemy has moved north of the Potomac in large force, push north, following him and attacking him wherever found; follow him if driven south of the Potomac as long as it is safe to do so.

There are now on the way to join you three other brigades of the best of cavalry, numbering at least 5,000 men and horses. These will be instructed, in the absence of further orders, to join you by the south side of the Potomac. In pushing up the Shenandoah Valley, where it is expected you will have to go first or last, it is desirable that nothing should be left to invite the enemy to return. Take all provisions, forage and stock wanted for the use of your command; such as cannot be consumed, destroy. It is not desirable that the buildings be destroyed; they should rather be protected, but the people should be informed that so long as an army can subsist among them recurrences of these raids must be expected, and we are determined to stop them at all hazards. Bear in mind the object is to drive the enemy south, and to do this you want to always keep him in sight. Be guided in your course by the course he takes.

(Signed) U. S. Grant,
Lieutenant-General."

Sheridan found Early's army concentrated west of the Opequon River, covering Winchester and Bunker Hill. He moved his own army from Halltown to a line running from Clifton to Berryville, sending part of his cavalry to White Post on the Front Royal road and posting the remainder under Lowell at Summit Point, on the Harper's Ferry and Winchester Railroad, to guard his right flank. From these positions a general advance was made westward to the Opequon, when it was ascertained by the cavalry on the White Post and Winchester road that Early was retreating toward Strasburg, where the Valley is narrowest and most favorable for defense. This was on the 11th of August, 1864. Sheridan followed to Cedar Creek and, through very brisk reconnoitering, developed Early's main line on Fisher's Hill, immediately south of Strasburg, strongly entrenched.

While in these relative positions on the 12th, Sheridan learned of a large force of Confederates approaching

Front Royal from Culpeper by way of Chester Gap, in the Blue Ridge, almost directly opposite his left flank and only fifteen miles from it. Sheridan's information about the approach of these Confederates was confirmed on the morning of the 14th, when a special messenger from Washington, who came by way of Snicker's Gap, brought the following dispatch from General Grant:

"City Point, August 12, 1864, 9 A. M.
Major-General Halleck:

Inform General Sheridan it is now certain two (2) divisions of infantry have gone to Early, and some cavalry and twenty (20) pieces of artillery. This movement commenced last Saturday night. He must be cautious and act on the defensive until movements here force them to detach to send this way. Early's force, with this increase, cannot exceed forty thousand men, but this is too much for General Sheridan to attack.
U. S. Grant,
Lieutenant-General."

To fully verify this information, Sheridan, on the 14th and 15th, sent Merritt's Division of cavalry to Front Royal and withdrew all his infantry to the north side of Cedar Creek, prior to withdrawing entirely to what Sheridan considered the best defensive position in the lower Valley—at Halltown and Harper's Ferry. By this movement he would also be marching toward reinforcements then coming to him from Washington by way of Snicker's Gap, of the Blue Ridge, and consisting of Grover's Division of the Nineteenth Corps and Wilson's Division of cavalry.

On the nights of the 15th and 16th he withdrew his entire infantry force to Winchester, leaving his cavalry out as a screen, but with instructions, as it retired, to carry out that part of General Grant's orders to destroy all stores and forage south of a line drawn westward from Millwood to Winchester and Petticoat Gap, in North Mountain. Also to seize all mules, horses and cattle that might be useful to his army. No houses were to be burned and the people were to be informed "that the object is to make this valley untenable for the raiding parties of the rebel army." The infantry was withdrawn at night, mainly because the movement could not be concealed during the day from Early's lookouts on Massanutten Mountain, overlooking the entire region about Strasburg and Cedar Creek.

This withdrawal was made none too soon, for on the afternoon of the 16th, before the main infantry had commenced to move back, Merritt's cavalry was attacked at the Shenandoah crossing of the Front Royal and Winchester road by Gen. R. H. Anderson's infantry, Kershaw's Division, and Fitzhugh Lee's two brigades of cavalry, arriving in the Valley from Richmond and Culpeper via Chester Gap. Merritt repulsed Anderson's attack, capturing two battle flags and three hundred prisoners, and then fell back to White Post, while the infantry was getting into position on the 17th at Berryville and Clifton, and Wilson's and

Lowell's cavalry held Winchester. Averell's Cavalry Division had returned to Hancock from Moorefield, where it had attacked and dispersed McCausland's Confederate cavalry on the 7th of August.

Early started in pursuit of Sheridan on the 17th, as soon as he became aware of the latter's retirement, driving the Federal cavalry out of Winchester toward Summit Point that same evening, Early being joined by Anderson's column near Winchester on the morning of the 18th. Sheridan then drew Merritt back from White Post to Berryville, while the cavalry on his other flank held a line from Summit Point, with pickets out along the Opequon, to Smithfield Bridge, the infantry being posted near Charlestown, where, on the 21st, Early made a reconnaissance in force by way of Smithfield Bridge, but quickly withdrew again west of the Opequon, and Sheridan then moved his entire army to Halltown, posting his cavalry on his right flank toward Shepherdstown.

This general retrograde movement from Strasburg to Halltown by Sheridan's army, leaving Maryland and Pennsylvania again open to Confederate raiding parties, caused intense commotion at the North and excitement at Washington, although, by keeping close contact with Early, Sheridan, from his position at Halltown or from Berryville, was able to closely follow after Early's army should the latter attempt to cross north of the Potomac, or, if he went east of the Blue Ridge toward Washington, Sheridan could readily interpose his army to protect the Capital. Still it was a retrograde movement, justified by the prudence of not risking a battle with a superior force at Cedar Creek, so far away from his base at Harper's Ferry, and with Anderson's reinforcements arriving at Front Royal on his left flank to threaten his communications to the rear.

Early felt Sheridan's lines at Halltown on the 22d and the following days, until the night of the 25th, when he retired west of the Opequon, concentrating his forces at Bunker Hill and Brucetown. Sheridan moved forward to Charlestown on the 28th and seized Smithfield Bridge with Merritt's Cavalry Division. On the 29th a heavy force of Confederate infantry first drove Merritt back toward Charlestown, and then, in turn, were driven out across the Opequon, which was thereafter held by Sheridan's cavalry.

Averell, who had been guarding the crossings of the Potomac from Hancock down the north side of the river to Antietam Creek, crossed to the south side and advanced to Martinsburg on the 29th, driving out the enemy's pickets; but Averell in turn was driven back to Falling Waters by Rodes's Division of infantry on the 31st. On the 2d of September Averell advanced again through Martinsburg to near Bunker Hill, where he attacked and routed Early's Cavalry (now commanded by Lomax, who had succeeded Ransom), capturing 2 battle-flags, 55 prisoners, some wagons and a herd of cattle, finally driving Lomax nearly into Winchester on the 3d.

On that day Sheridan moved his infantry to a line running from Clifton to Berryyille, his cavalry (except Averell's Division) being pushed south to White Post. Averell was brought east of the Opequon to Leetown. There was virtually no change in these positions until the 19th of September.

Information had been received a fortnight before, that Kershaw's Division of infantry had been or was to be ordered to return to Richmond, where Grant's activity was causing Lee great concern. Lee had already recalled Hampton's Cavalry Division when it was marching to join Anderson at Culpeper on the 14th of August. Kershaw's Division of infantry, with Gen. R. H. Anderson, finally left Winchester on the 14th of September to return to General Lee via Front Royal; by Early's advice he had already made an attempt on the 3d to go through to Millwood and Ashby's Gap into Loudoun County, for the purpose of giving the appearance of moving on Washington, but on that occasion he had unexpectedly run into Crook's Corps near Berryville, and, after a sharp engagement, returned to Winchester. Everything then being quiet, and at the repeated summons from General Lee that at least he and his staff should return to Richmond to resume command of the First Army Corps, Anderson started again from Winchester with Kershaw's Division, as above seen.

This was what Sheridan claims to have been waiting for to assume the offensive against Early; General Grant, having come from City Point to Charlestown on the 16th of September, approved Sheridan's plans of attack and then returned to the Army of the Potomac. At 3 A. M. of the 19th, Sheridan's army moved out from the Clifton-Berry ville line to the Opequon, Wilson's cavalry first striking Ramseur's Confederate Division immediately west of the Opequon in the canyon on the Berryville-Winchester road, driving it in toward Winchester. This movement was supported by the Sixth and Nineteenth Corps, who, with Crook's Eighth Corps in reserve, then took up the fighting, which became desperate, with varying results throughout the day, until Crook's Corps, having been put in on the right of the Nineteenth Corps, found the enemy's left flank and crushed it. Simultaneously the two Divisions of cavalry (Merritt's and Averell's) under Torbert, which had crossed the Opequon lower down (north) and had joined forces at Stephenson's Depot, came charging up the Martinsburg road, driving before them Lomax's Confederate Cavalry Division in a confused mass through the Confederate broken infantry troops. Sheridan then advanced his entire infantry line, and assembling Torbert's two Cavalry Divisions on the right of the infantry, directed them to renew the charge, and Early's army was driven through Winchester hopelessly routed at dark, in full retreat toward Newtown and Fisher's Hill, where the valley narrows down to about four miles in width and furnishes an almost impregnable defensive position, which Early had also strongly entrenched.

The losses at the Battle of the Opequon (or Winchester) were: Union, killed, 697; wounded, 3,983; missing, 338—total, 5,018. Confederates; Early's official report gives his killed at 226, wounded, 1,567; missing, 1,818—total, 3,611, and he also admits losing three guns, but makes no report of his cavalry losses, which were undoubtedly heavy. Among general officers lost were Generals Rodes and Godwin by the Confederates; Gen. D. A. Russell by the Federals—all killed.

On the 31st of August Sheridan's returns showed a strength present of about 50,000 men, of whom 8,000 were cavalry. It is not possible to get at Early's strength for the same period, on account of the incompleteness of his returns, and want of mention of either his artillery or his cavalry, but his army was undoubtedly inferior in all arms to Sheridan's, especially in cavalry.

Sheridan, on the 20th of September, followed Early with his infantry and Merritt's cavalry on the Valley turnpike to the Heights of Strasburg, sending his cavalry under Averell by a parallel road to the westward, known as the Back road, and Wilson's cavalry eastward toward Front Royal by a road diverging from the Valley pike at Newtown. During the night of the 21st orders were sent to Crook's Corps to repeat his movement of the 19th, by getting into position on the Confederate left flank and attacking from that direction. To do so, Crook was moved from his position in reserve on Cedar Creek to a point on North Mountain, some distance beyond where Sheridan had massed the Nineteenth and the Sixth Army Corps, then passing through a series of ravines and woods, which concealed his movements, to a point which brought him in beyond the Confederate left. Crook, early on the 226, formed in two parallel columns and proceeded in that formation until he had gone almost the length of his columns to the rear of the Confederate entrenchments, when he faced to the left, and thus formed a double line of battle, which was moved forward with a shout, going over very difficult ground and taking the Confederate battle-lined entrenchments in reverse, driving out its defenders in confusion, who were pursued four miles without being permitted to reform. A battery near the left of the Confederate line was abandoned by its gunners and run over by Crook's men, and small arms in great quantities were thrown away. Being then joined by Ricketts's Division of the Sixth Corps, which, equally with all the remainder of the infantry, had passed through the Confederate lines in their front, Crook continued the pursuit until dark. Crook's losses were only 8 killed, 153 wounded and 1 missing. The entire losses were but 528. Among those Crook thanked in his official report, was Capt. William McKinley, acting assistant adjutant-general.

At Fisher's Hill Early reported his losses to aggregate 1,235 men and 12 guns, and many small arms thrown away. In taking up that position, which had been repaired and strengthened a month before, Early evidently expected to check effectually Sheridan's jubilant army from passing farther south up the Valley. To secure himself at Fisher's Hill and his communications with Harrisonburg and Staunton, Early immediately detached Fitzhugh Lee's cavalry on the 20th of September to prevent any movement of the enemy into the Luray Valley by way of Front Royal. There Fitzhugh Lee was attacked by Sheridan's cavalry under Torbert on the 21st and again at Milford Creek on the 22d. At the latter place the Shenandoah impinges so closely upon the Blue Ridge that the position could not be turned, and the banks of Milford Creek so precipitous that a direct attack was out of the question; so, on the 23d, Torbert withdrew to Front Royal, Cedarville and Buckton. There he learned of the victory at Fisher's Hill, and at the same time received orders from Sheridan to move up the Luray Valley again. Torbert found the enemy had gone from Milford Creek, but came up with him on the 24th, three miles from Luray, driving him through the town and out on the New Market road over Massanutten Mountain. On the 25th Torbert rejoined the main army at New Market, Early having retreated through that place the day before, and gone through Harrisonburg to Port Republic, in which direction he was followed by Torbert's cavalry, who also sent a part of his force around through Staunton to Waynesborough. Here Torbert met resistance from Early's main army and fell back toward Staunton on the night of the 28th, to Spring Hill, on Middle River, and went to Bridgewater, on North River, on the 29th. The other part of Torbert's cavalry was at Cross Keys operating in the vicinity of Brown's Gap and Piedmont. Early, meanwhile, had been reinforced by Kershaw's Division of infantry, which had been diverted by General Lee at Orange Court House, while it was marching to rejoin him at Richmond pursuant to previous orders already mentioned. Kershaw joined Early at Port Republic. Rosser, with his brigade of cavalry, was also sent to Early via Burksville.

Sheridan moved his infantry to Harrisonburg on the 25th and to Mount Crawford on the 29th, while Torbert's cavalry were carrying out General Grant's instructions to destroy all mills, grain, forage, etc., that they could not use themselves, in the vicinity of Staunton, Waynesboro, Piedmont and Port Republic. Grant's latest orders to Sheridan of September 26 read: "If the war is to last another year, we want the Shenandoah Valley 10 remain a barren waste."

It was while at Harrisonburg on the 1st of October that Sheridan received a dispatch from General Grant, dated September 28, and sent through General Halleck at Washington, that it was expected of him to reach Charlottesville. Sheridan, in reply, said: "It is no easy matter to pass these mountain gaps [meaning the Blue Ridge] and attack Charlottesville, hauling supplies through difficult passes, 14 miles in length, and with a line of communication from 135 to 145 miles long, without the organization of supply trains, ordnance trains, and all the appointments of an army making a permanent advance. I am ready and willing to cross the Blue Ridge, but know from present indications that the enemy will strongly fortify at Charlottesville and Gordonsville, and that these places cannot be taken without the expenditure of a largely superior force to keep open the line of communication. With my present means I cannot accumulate supplies enough to carry me through to the Orange and Alexandria Railroad."

In a dispatch to Halleck of the same date as the one to Grant (October 1, 1864,) Sheridan says: "I strongly advise General Grant to terminate this campaign by the destruction of the crops in the Valley and the means of planting, and the transfer of the Sixth and Nineteenth Corps to his army at Richmond. This is my best judgment. With Crook's force the Valley can be held. There is no objective point except Lynchburg, and it cannot be invested on the line of this Valley and the investing army supplied. What we have destroyed and can destroy in this Valley is worth millions of dollars to the rebel Government."

On the 3d of October General Grant telegraphed Secretary Stanton: "I will follow Sheridan's suggestion of bringing the Sixth and Nineteenth Corps here and yours as to bringing them by rail from Front Royal."
So General Grant relinquished for the time his pet idea of getting possession of Charlottesville and breaking up the Virginia Central Railroad at that point. He had urged that movement on Hunter when that officer was on his expedition up the Valley towards Lynchburg in June, and had sent Sheridan with two divisions of cavalry from City Point to meet Hunter in that vicinity when Sheridan was intercepted by Wade Hampton at Trevilians's. Grant repeated the project to Hunter and to Wright after Early had retreated from in front of Washington, and we have just

seen how he recurred to the same plan when Sheridan reached Harrisonburg and Staunton.

On the 3d of October Grant directed Sheridan: "Take up such position in the Valley as you think can and ought to be held, and send all the force not required for this immediately here. Leave nothing for the subsistence of an army on any ground you abandon to the enemy. I will direct the railroad to be pushed toward Front Royal, so that you may send your troops back that way." As the Manassas Gap Railroad from Strasburg and Front Royal would carry the troops to Alexandria, water transportation from that place to City Point was arranged for.

With this authority Sheridan commenced withdrawing from the upper Valley on the 6th of October, his cavalry moving in rear of his infantry and stretched "across the Valley from the Blue Ridge to the eastern slope of the Alleghenies, with directions to burn all forage and drive off all stock, etc., as they moved to the rear, fully coinciding with the views of the Lieutenant-General, that the Valley should be made a barren waste. The most positive orders were given, however, not to burn private dwellings. In this movement the enemy's cavalry followed at a respectful distance until in the vicinity of Woodstock, when they attacked Custer's Division, and harassed it as far as Tom's Brook, a short distance south of Fisher's Hill."

There, on the 8th of October, Sheridan halted his infantry and instructed Torbert to engage the Confederate cavalry and to defeat it. With Custer's Division on the Back road and Merritt's on the Valley pike, the heads of the opposing columns came in contact at Tom's Brook on the 9th and deployed. "After a short but decisive engagement the enemy was defeated, with the loss of all his artillery, excepting one piece, and everything else that was carried on wheels. The rout was complete and was followed up to Mount Jackson, a distance of some twenty-six miles.

"On October 10th the army crossed to the north side of Cedar Creek, the Sixth Corps continuing its march to Front Royal." From this the Sixth Corps was recalled, however, when it was learned that Early's army had returned to his entrenched lines on Fisher's Hill on the 13th.

While Sheridan was at Harrisonburg and above, it was found to be exceedingly difficult to get the necessary supply trains through to him from Martinsburg or Harper's Ferry, unless heavily escorted. It was simply a repetition of the experience of Banks and Fremont in 1862 and of Hunter in June, 1864, while operating in that same region, among a thoroughly hostile population, with Mosby's and White's men swarming through the passes of the Blue Ridge from Loudoun County to fall upon any unprotected convoy that could not be fought through. With Sheridan the case was made more difficult still, by the addition of hundreds of armed stragglers from Early's army who had been dispersed at the battles of Winchester and Fisher's Hill, and who, under the leadership of their officers, likewise stragglers, had been gathered from the mountains in squads, after Sheridan's army had passed on, and formed in the aggregate quite a formidable force in his rear.

While on his return march, Sheridan reports to Grant from Woodstock on the 7th of October the results of his operations as follows: "In moving back to this point the whole country from the Blue Ridge to the North Mountains has been made untenable for a rebel army. I have destroyed over 2,000 barns filled with wheat, hay and farming implements; over 70 mills filled with flour and wheat; have driven in front of the army over 4,000 head of stock, and have killed and issued to the troops not less than 3,000 sheep. This destruction embraces the Luray Valley and Little Fort Valley, as well as the main Valley. A large number of horses have been obtained, a proper estimate of which I cannot now make. Since I came into the Valley from Harper's Ferry up to Harrisonburg, every train, every small party and every straggler has been bushwhacked by people, many of whom have protection papers from commanders who have been hitherto in this Valley.

From the vicinity of Harrisonburg over 400 wagon loads of refugees have been sent back to Martinsburg; most of these people were Dunkers and had been conscripted.

To-morrow I will continue the destruction of wheat, forage, etc., down to Fisher's Hill. When this is completed, the Valley from Winchester up to Staunton, ninety-two miles, will have but little in it for man or beast."

These Dunkers are a religious sect which came to America from Switzerland and Germany between 1719 and 1729; they settled first in Pennsylvania, from where they spread out into Ohio, Maryland and Virginia. Their belief was akin both to that of the Baptists and the Friends, particularly that tenet of the latter sect which forbids the shedding of human blood in battle.

Being essentially an agricultural people, the fertile valley of the Shenandoah was not long in inviting them to settle there the overflow from their increasing numbers in Pennsylvania, especially from the Cumberland Valley, by way of its physical extension southward across the Potomac through Winchester, up to the broad expanse of the Valley at Harrisonburg and vicinity.

It was the descendants of these Dunker pioneers that Sheridan found means to provide for, when he loaded them into his empty wagons at Harrisonburg and brought them North with him. His orders had required him to destroy their means of subsistence and leave them destitute, so that Confederate troops could no longer forage there.

The relations of the Dunkers to the Confederacy were passive rather than disloyal. They meekly accepted the situation and the usual conditions of war, except to volunteer to bear arms and go into battle. This their religious faith forbade.

They submitted to all the penalties of the Conscription Acts, but still refused to shed blood,—until modified relief came to them through an Act of the Confederate Congress, dated October 11, 1862, by which provision was made to exempt them as follows: "... and all persons who have been or who are now members of the Society of Friends and the Association of Dunkards, Nazarenes, and Mennonites, in regular membership in their respective denominations, provided, [they] shall furnish substitutes or pay a tax of five hundred dollars each into the public Treasury."

A more liberal Act of the Legislature of Virginia had already been passed March 29th, 1862, by which there was a proviso that, where unable to pay the tax of five hundred dollars, a Dunkard might "be employed as a teamster or in some character which will not require the actual bearing of arms," etc.

To the westward of the Valley, about Wardensville and Moorefield, there were two bodies of partisans, under the leadership of Harness and McNeill, who were very enterprising, and constantly making forays through that mountainous section toward the Baltimore and Ohio Railroad near Cumberland or New Creek (Keyser), or up the South Branch Valley.

But the most formidable of all the independent parties of Confederate regulars or irregulars sent out that season, was one organized under Lieut.-Col. Vincent A. Witcher, of the Thirty-fourth Battalion Virginia Cavalry, which, starting from Jeffersonville, in Southwestern Virginia, passed down the Valley of New River to Lewisburg, where Witcher picked up several small guerilla bands commanded by the Thurmond brothers and others, making an aggregate force of 523.

Leaving Lewisburg on the 22d of September, Witcher marched northward over the Cold Knob trail to Bulltown; thence position at Winchester, mainly to operate against Mosby and White, east of the Blue Ridge, and against Harry Gilmor or the McNeills in the vicinity of Moorefield, to the westward in the South Branch of the Potomac Valley.

In one of these latter Harry Gilmor was surprised in bed at Randolph's, three miles out from Moorefield, at an early hour of the 5th of February. Gilmor, who appeared to be a freelance partisan from Maryland, had been sent by Early to take charge of the McNeill and Harness bands, operating near Moorefield, who resisted all control by anybody (especially by Gilmor).

Sheridan in his "Memoirs" says of Gilmor's capture: "Thus the last link between Maryland and the Confederacy was carried a prisoner to Winchester, whence he was sent to Fort Warren." The capture was effected by Colonel Young and twenty men of Sheridan's scouts, dressed in Confederate uniforms, supported by a mixed cavalry detachment of 300 men under Lieut.-Col. E. W. Whitaker, First Connecticut Cavalry. As an offset to this capture of Gilmor, a party of 50 of his men, led by young Jesse McNeill and dressed in Federal uniforms, entered the City of Cumberland during the night of the 21st of February, proceeded direct to the hotel which was the headquarters of both Generals Kelley and Crook, surprising them in bed. Not a shot was fired and so little disturbance created, that staff officers living in rooms adjoining those of Generals Crook and Kelley, were not awakened.

The raiders remained only ten minutes in the town, and then hastily withdrew on the Springfield and Romney road with their prisoners, reaching Staunton in the upper Shenandoah on the 24th—all efforts to intercept the party having failed.

These captures were even more daringly made than was that of Harry Gilmor, about a fortnight earlier in the month, by Colonel Young.

On the 27th of February, 1865, Sheridan started from Winchester with two divisions of cavalry (Custer's and Devin's) and three sections of artillery, the whole commanded by Major-General Wesley Merritt. The strength of the force was 9,987 officers and men.

The men carried five days' rations in haversacks, with fifteen days' additional rations of coffee, sugar and salt in wagons, thirty pounds of forage for each horse, one wagon for each division headquarters, eight ambulances and an ammunition train. No other wagons were allowed except a pontoon train of eight boats.

According to the instructions of General Grant, Sheridan was to destroy the Virginia Central Railroad, the James River canal, capture Lynchburg, if practicable, and then join General Sherman wherever he might be found in North Carolina, or return to Winchester.

Sheridan's troops were in fine condition for the movement, notwithstanding the bad condition of the roads and the continued inclemency of the weather, Early's depleted command near Staunton promising little opposition.

Staunton was reached in four marches and found abandoned by the enemy, who had withdrawn eastward to Waynesboro. He was closely followed and assaulted in position by Custer's Division, March 2d, who charged around and over the breastworks of Early's two brigades of infantry, dispersing them as well as a small body of cavalry under Rosser. The pursuit of the fugitives was continued as far as the South Fork of the Shenandoah River, where n pieces of artillery, with horses and caissons complete, 200 loaded wagons, 17 battle flags and 1,400 officers and men were captured. Generals Early, Long, Wharton, Lilley and Rosser, with a few men, escaped.

From Waynesboro the prisoners and captured artillery were sent back to Winchester under escort of 1,600 men, who safely reached their destination, although constantly harassed by a considerable force which Rosser had succeeded in gathering.

Meanwhile Custer pushed on to Charlottesville, destroying much government property on the way, besides the railroad and its bridges. At 4 p. m. of the 3d of March he was met by the mayor and prominent citizens of Charlottesville, that town so long coveted by General Grant, who surrendered the place peaceably.

Wharton, who had gathered a few of his infantry at Charlottesville the day before Custer's arrival, endeavored to find Early, but the latter with a small party had fled eastward toward Richmond.

With this dispersal of Early's army at Waynesboro, campaigns in the Shenandoah were ended.

Some minor scouting expeditions against Mosby's partisans were made from the region of Winchester, where Sheridan had left behind two or three thousand men to protect the lower valley. The line of the Baltimore and Ohio Railroad and of the Potomac River, from Harper's Ferry westward, were strongly held against possible raiding parties coming either from the direction of the country where Mosby continued to operate, or from the region of Moorefield, where Jesse McNeill still had a small following.

When Sheridan moved south from Winchester, President Lincoln showed some concern that Washington might be uncovered from that direction, but he was reassured by General Grant, who sent Hancock to command, during Sheridan's absence, all the territory comprised within the Middle Military Division, from Washington west to the Ohio River. Hancock's headquarters were fixed at Cumberland.

From Charlottesville Sheridan subsequently moved to the White House on the Pamunkey, and thence to the south side of the James, where he joined Grant and was placed by him on the extreme left of his army. That part of his instructions to capture Lynchburg and then strike out to join Sherman's army coming north through North Carolina, Sheridan found to be impracticable, on account of the very high stage of water in the James from Lynchburg down, all bridges having been destroyed and his eight pontoons being insufficient to effect a crossing.to Weston and Buckhannon. The only resistance Witcher mentioned having was from some home-guards at each of the abovementioned places, who were easily dispersed. He claims to have captured and paroled 300 prisoners, taken 1,000 small arms, 400 horses and 300 beef cattle, and destroyed large quantities of commissary, quartermaster and medical stores. General Lee had authorized the expedition and commended the results, but it had no military value beyond causing a commotion to the weak guards of the Baltimore and Ohio Railroad within General Kelley's jurisdiction, west of Cumberland, although none of Witcher's men reached the railroad itself. The movement was intended by General Lee as a diversion in favor of Early, but Witcher found the railroad too well guarded to be attacked, so he withdrew to the Greenbrier country. The excesses committed by Witcher's men were so discreditable that the Confederate War Department was forced to take notice of them.

———

CHAPTER XII
Sheridan's Campaigns (Continued)
Battle of Cedar Creek and Subsequent Cavalry Movements

That the project of a movement on Gordonsville still existed in General Grant's mind was made manifest by a dispatch from Halleck to Sheridan, dated Washington, October 12, noon, reading: "General Grant wishes a position taken far enough south to serve as a base for future operations upon Gordonsville and Charlottesville. It must be strongly fortified and provisioned. Some point in the vicinity of Manassas Gap would seem best suited for all purposes." It is to be recalled that a large force of men and a railroad construction corps were at work restoring the Manassas Gap Railroad from Alexandria (or Manassas Junction) through to Front Royal, although continually harassed by Mosby's and White's guerrilla bands. The expectation was to transfer Sheridan's base of supplies from Harper's Ferry to Alexandria as soon as the Manassas Gap Railroad could be made use of.

This revived Gordonsville project Sheridan disapproved of, and after considerable communication backward and forward between him and Washington, and Washington with City Point, he was called to Washington by Mr. Stanton on the 13th of October, who said: "If you can come here a consultation on several points is extremely desirable. I propose to visit General Grant and would like to see you first."

Early, who had been reinforced by Kershaw's Infantry Division at Port Republic, September 26th and by Rosser's Cavalry Division on the 2d of October at Mount Crawford, followed Sheridan's forces as the latter retired down the valley, Early halting his infantry for a few days at New Market, and then moving down to his old line at Fisher's Hill on the 13th of October, as already stated, closely observant of Sheridan's further movements.

In his general report of the Valley campaigns, which he wrote at New Orleans February 3, 1866, Sheridan says: "On the evening of the 15th I determined to go [meaning to Washington], believing that the enemy at Fisher's Hill could not accomplish much, and as I had concluded not to attack him at present, I ordered the whole of the cavalry force under General Torbert to accompany me to Front Royal, from where I intended to push it through Chester Gap to the Virginia Central Railroad at Charlottesville, while I passed through Manassas Gap to Piedmont, thence by rail to Washington. Upon my arrival with the cavalry at Front Royal on the night of the 16th, I received a dispatch from General Wright, who was left at Cedar Creek in command of the army, to the effect that a message taken off the Confederate signal flag on Three Top Mountain, overlooking Fisher's Hill, indicated that Longstreet was moving to Early's support, and when the two forces joined they would crush Sheridan. Moreover, Wright expressed great uneasiness that the enemy might attack his right flank from the direction of North Mountain."

Sheridan then says concerning the Confederate signal message: "My first thought was that it was a ruse, but, on reflection, deemed it best to abandon the cavalry raid and give to Wright the entire strength of the army. I therefore ordered the cavalry to return and report to him."

Sheridan then rode on to Piedmont, where he found transportation to Washington by rail, reaching that city on the morning of the 17th; had his interview with Mr. Stanton and returned to Winchester by a special train over the Baltimore and Ohio as far as Martinsburg, so that he reached Winchester on the night of the 18th of October and slept there.

Torbert's two divisions of cavalry, meanwhile, had rejoined Wright from Front Royal on the 17th, one division (Powell's) being placed along the line of the Shenandoah from the left of the army toward Front Royal, while Merritt's division returned to its former position on the right of the infantry, where Custer's Division had remained to cover that flank, during the absence of the other two divisions, when Sheridan organized the projected raid on Charlottesville via Front Royal and Chester Gap, which he subsequently abandoned.

So that, on the night of the 18th, the line of the Union Army was along Cedar Creek, the Eighth Corps (Crook's) on the left, with Powell's Cavalry Division to his left, but about eight miles away at the crossing of the Shenandoah on the Front Royal and Winchester turnpike. To the right of Crook came the Nineteenth Army Corps, then commanded by Emory, and still farther to the right was the Sixth Corps (Wright's). Merritt's and Custer's Cavalry Divisions were placed beyond the right of the Sixth Corps, and west of Middletown. The general direction of the entire line was originally S. E. to N. W., north of Cedar Creek.

Early, in his report of October 21 to General Lee from New Market, says:

"After ascertaining the location of the enemy's camps by observation from the signal station on Massanutten Mountain, I determined to move around the left flank of the enemy. To get around the enemy's left was a very difficult undertaking, however, as the river had to be crossed twice, and between the mountain and river, where the troops had to pass to the lower ford, there was only a rugged pathway. I thought, however, the chances of success would be greater from the fact that the enemy would not expect a move in that direction, on account of the difficulties attending it and the great strength of their position on that flank. The movement was accordingly begun on the night of the 18th just after dark, Gordon's, Ramseur's and Pegram's Divisions being sent across the river and around the foot of the mountain, all under command of General Gordon; and late at night I moved with Kershaw's Division through Strasburg toward a ford on Cedar Creek just above its mouth, and Wharton was moved on the pike toward the enemy's front, in which road the artillery was also moved. The arrangement was for Gordon to come around in the rear, for Kershaw to attack the left flank, and for Wharton to advance in front, supporting the artillery, which was to open on the enemy when he should turn on Gordon or Kershaw, and the attack was to begin at 5 A. M.

Rosser was sent to the left to occupy the enemy's cavalry, and Lomax, who had been sent down the Luray Valley, was ordered to pass Front Royal, cross the river and move across to the Valley pike.

Punctually at 5 A. M. Kershaw reached the enemy's left work and attacked and carried it without the least difficulty, and very shortly afterwards Gordon attacked in the rear, and they swept everything before them, routing the Eighth and Nineteenth Corps completely, getting possession of their camp and capturing 18 pieces of artillery and about 1,300 prisoners. They moved across the pike toward the camp of the Sixth Corps, and Wharton was crossed over, the artillery following him; but the Sixth Corps, which was on the enemy's extreme right of his infantry, was not surprised in camp, because Rosser had commenced the attack on that flank about the same time as the attack on the other, and the firing on the left gave that corps sufficient time to form and move out of camp, and it was found posted on a ridge on the west of the pike and parallel to it, and this corps offered considerable resistance. The artillery was brought up and opened on it, when it fell back to the north of Middletown and made a stand on a commanding ridge running across the pike.

In the meantime the enemy's cavalry was threatening our right flank and rear, and the country being perfectly open, and having on that flank only Lomax's old brigade, numbering about 300 men. it became necessary to make dispositions to prevent a cavalry charge and a portion of the troops were moved to the right for that purpose, and word was sent to Gordon, who had got on the left with his division, and Kershaw, who was there also, to swing round and advance with their divisions; but they stated in reply that a heavy force of cavalry had got in their front, and that their ranks were so depleted by the number of men who had stopped in the camps to plunder, that they could not advance them.

Rosser also sent word that when he attacked the cavalry he found a part of the Sixth Corps supporting it; that a very heavy force of cavalry had massed in his front and that it was too strong for him and that he would have to fall back. I sent word to him to get some position that he could hold, and the cavalry in front of Kershaw and Gordon having moved toward Rosser, they were moved forward and a line was formed north of Middletown and facing the enemy. The cavalry on the right made several efforts to charge that flank but was driven back.

So many of our men had stopped in the camp to plunder (in which I am sorry to say that officers participated), the country was so open and the enemy's cavalry was so strong, that I did not deem it prudent to press further, especially as Lomax had not come up. I determined, therefore, to content myself with trying to hold the advantages I had gained until all my troops had come up and the captured property was secured. If I had had but one division of fresh troops I could have made the victory complete and beyond all danger of a reverse. We continued to hold our position until late in the afternoon when the enemy commenced advancing."

In the Union army the first blow had fallen upon the left flank and rear of Crook's Eighth Army Corps (the Army of West Virginia), then numbering about 4,000 men present, and constituting the left of the Federal infantry forces. This corps was soon crushed back upon the Nineteenth Corps, which, in turn, was fiercely attacked by the Confederates from the rear and on both flanks, and after some resistance forced from its position, and both corps being overpowered, were seized with panic and dispersed toward Middletown, north of which place a rally was finally made upon the unbroken Sixth Corps (Wright's) about 1 p. M., and further attacks by the enemy successfully resisted. It was at this stage that General Sheridan reached the field from Winchester, ten miles away, and resumed command of the disordered army, General Wright, on whom the command had devolved during Sheridan's absence, returning to his own, the Sixth Corps.

Sheridan in his report of the battle says: "At about 7 o'clock on the morning of the 19th of October an officer on picket at Winchester reported artillery firing, but, supposing it resulted from a reconnaissance which had been ordered for this morning, I paid no attention to it and was unconscious of the true condition of affairs until about 9 o'clock, when, having ridden through the town of Winchester, the sound of artillery made a battle unmistakable, and, on reaching Mill Creek, half a mile south of Winchester, the head of the fugitives appeared in sight, trains and men coming to the rear with appalling rapidity. I immediately gave directions to halt and park the trains at Mill Creek, and ordered the brigade at Winchester to stretch across the country and stop all stragglers. Taking twenty men from my escort I pushed on to the front. I am happy to say that hundreds of the men, when on reflection found they had not done themselves justice, came back with cheers.

On arriving at the front I found Merritt's and Custer's Divisions of Cavalry, under Torbert, and General Getty's Division of the Sixth Corps, opposing the enemy. I suggested to General Wright that we would fight on Getty's line, and to transfer Custer to the right at once, as he (Custer) and Merritt, from being on the right in the morning, had been transferred to the left; that the remaining two divisions of the Sixth Corps, which were to the right and rear of Getty about two miles, should be ordered up, and also that the Nineteenth Corps, which was on the right and rear of these two divisions, should be hastened up before the enemy attacked Getty. I then started out all my staff officers to bring up these troops, and was so convinced that we would soon be attacked that I went back myself to urge them on. Immediately after I returned and assumed command, General Wright returning to his corps, Getty to his division, the line of battle was formed on the prolongation of Getty's line, and a temporary breastwork of rails, logs, etc., thrown up hastily. At 4 p. m. I ordered the advance. It was at this stage of the battle that Custer was ordered to charge with his entire division, but, although the order was promptly obeyed, it was not in time to capture the whole of the force thus cut off, and many escaped across Cedar Creek. Simultaneous with this charge a combined movement of the whole line drove the enemy in confusion to the creek, where, owing to the difficulties of crossing, his army became routed. Custer, finding a ford on Cedar Creek west of the pike, and Devin, of Merritt's Division, one to the east of it, they each made a crossing just after dark and pursued the routed mass of the enemy to Fisher's Hill, where his strong position gave him some protection against our cavalry; but most of his transportation had been captured, the road from Cedar Creek to Fisher's Hill, a distance of over three miles, being literally blockaded by wagons, ambulances, artillery, caissons, etc."

For the harrowing particulars of that rout, the loss of artillery and transportation, etc., Early gives in his report to General Lee a most graphic and pathetic account of the crumbling away of his infantry under Sheridan's attack, commencing on the left of his line in Gordon's Division, followed by Kershaw's and Ramseur's; "when they found Gordon's giving away, not because there was any pressure on them, but because of an insane idea of being flanked. Some of them, however, were rallied, and with the help of the artillery the army [enemy] was checked for some time; but a great number of the men could not be stopped, but continued to go to the rear. The left again gave way, and then the whole command falling back in such a panic that I had to order Pegram's and Wharton's commands, which were very small and on the right, to fall back, and most of them took the panic also. I found it impossible to rally the troops. They would not listen to entreaties, threats, or appeals of any kind. A terror of the enemy's cavalry had seized them and there was no holding them. They left the field in the greatest confusion. All the captured artillery had been carried across Cedar Creek and a large number of captured wagons and ambulances, and we succeeded in crossing our own artillery over. A small body of the enemy's cavalry dashed across Cedar Creek above the bridge and got into the train and artillery running back on the pike, and passed through our men to this side of Strasburg, tore up a bridge, and thus succeeded in capturing the greater part of the artillery and a number of ordnance and medical wagons and ambulances. The men scattered on the sides and the rout was as thorough and disgraceful as ever happened to our army."

Early claims to have captured 18 guns and 1,300 prisoners in the early part of the day; he secured his prisoners before the panic struck his troops, but his "net" loss in artillery on the 19th was 23 pieces. He does not give his own losses in prisoners, killed or wounded. As none of his division commanders made any reports that are now available, those losses will probably never be ascertained.

Sheridan gives his losses for the battles of the Opequon, September 19th, Fisher's Hill, September 22d, and Cedar Creek, October 19th, 1864, besides reconnaissance and minor engagements, as follows: Killed, 1,938; wounded, n,893; missing, 3,121—an aggregate of 16,952.

His field return for September 10, 1864, showed a strength of 40,672.

There is no record of Early's strength or of his losses during the 1864 campaign in the Valley.

It was several days before Sheridan could give many particulars of his victory at Cedar Creek, but on the 25th of October he telegraphed to General Grant as follows:

"The battle of the 19th still increases in results. We captured 48 pieces of artillery, caissons, horses and all the appointments; 24 of the above number were captured from us in the morning; these I returned, and in addition allowed the batteries to refit and exchange, and have left 24 pieces of rebel artillery, with caissons complete, which I will send to Washington to-morrow. All the ambulances of the Nineteenth Corps captured by the enemy were retaken, with 56 rebel ambulances in good condition, and as many more were destroyed. A number of wagons and ambulances were burned unnecessarily by the cavalry in the excitement. Not less than 300 wagons and ambulances were captured or burned. The road between Cedar Creek and Fisher's Hill for three miles was blocked by captured artillery and wagons. We captured 14 battle-flags. We are now reduced to an effective force of not over 22,000 infantry. From the accounts of officers, Early's infantry when he attacked me was 25,000; the number of cavalry not yet known."

This peculiar battle of Cedar Creek, or Belle Grove as the Confederates called it, probably has never had its exact counterpart. Early gives his reason for attacking an intrenched enemy, who was probably his superior in strength, that owing to the lack of forage for his animals and the great difficulty of otherwise supplying his troops, so far from his base, the intermediate country having been laid waste, he would be forced soon to withdraw his army altogether unless he could accomplish by surprise what he dared not attempt otherwise. He selected also the stronger flank of his enemy for the execution of his well-conceived plan, with success almost within his grasp, when, by superhuman efforts on the part of his enemy, together with the disintegration of his own troops, while plundering the captured Federal camps, the tide was turned against him. An hour more of daylight would have destroyed entirely his panic-stricken army. He found he could not rally his forces in his old entrenchments at Fisher's Hill, they having lost all organization, so under cover of the night he retreated to New Market, fortunately for him unpursued, while Sheridan's army simply returned for the night to the camps they had lost in the morning.

All reports show that no Confederate attack was expected, for even General Sheridan believed he could safely leave his army to obey Mr. Stanton's call to Washington, although the false Confederate signal message from Longstreet caused him great uneasiness.

Wright, whom he left in command, says that the reconnaissance by a brigade sent out from Crook's command returned on the 18th and reported "that nothing was to be found in his old camp (the enemy's), and that he had doubtless retreated up the valley." That reconnaissance could not have proceeded very far, for Crook's line, as shown by both Confederate and Union maps, was less than five miles from Early's. Not being satisfied with the result of this reconnaissance of the 18th, Wright prepared two others—one brigade from the Nineteenth Corps and another from the cavalry—to start at early dawn of the 19th of October, up the Valley turnpike and the Back road respectively, to ascertain the enemy's whereabouts. Both these columns were in the act of starting when the attack opened on both flanks of the army.

Wright expected an attack on his right flank instead of the left flank, if the enemy attacked him at all, for he said in his despatch of the 16th to Sheridan, then at Front Royal, transmitting the bogus signal message: "If the enemy should be strongly reinforced in cavalry, he might, by turning our right, give us a great deal of trouble. I shall hold on here until the enemy's movements are developed, and shall only fear an attack on my right, which I shall make every effort for guarding against and resisting."

After the battle of Cedar Creek and until the 10th of November, Early remained with his shattered army in the vicinity of New Market and Harrisonburg, reorganizing and recruiting his forces. He received during this period some accessions by conscripts, detailed men, and men of the second class (farmers).

At sunrise of the 10th of November Early marched his army from New Market down the Valley again, through Woodstock, and the next day to Middletown, where Sheridan's cavalry pickets were first encountered, the latter's main army being entrenched north of Newtown, at Kernstown, etc., where Sheridan had withdrawn shortly after the battle of Cedar Creek, to shorten his line of supplies from his depots at Winchester. Early lay in line of battle near Newtown on the 12th, but made no attack; his cavalry on both flanks were driven back, Rosser by Custer on the Back road as far as Cedar Creek and McCausland on the Front Royal road by Powell as far as Milford. Sheridan says of this movement: "In consequence of contradictory information received from scouts and captured cavalry prisoners, I was unconvinced of any rebel infantry being in my vicinity until it was too late to overtake it in its galloping retreat, a retreat which was continued until in the vicinity of Lacey's Spring, near Harrisonburg."

This affair was reported by Early to General Lee on the 13th from New Market, where he returned with his entire army, which he had taken with him to Newtown to ascertain Sheridan's location; he remained in the vicinity of New Market until December 16, meanwhile detaching Rosser's Cavalry Division on the 26th of November for a raid on Moorefield and New Creek. Kershaw's division of infantry had already been detached on the 15th of November and sent to Richmond by way of Staunton. On the 16th of December Early also sent to Richmond, Gordon's and Pegram's Divisions of infantry by way of Staunton and Waynesboro.

Early then had left with him but two divisions of infantry (Wharton's and Rodes's, or Grimes's) and Rosser's and Lomax's Divisions of cavalry, which were then retired up the valley from New Market on the 16th of December, Wharton and Grimes going to Fishersville, while Lomax went to Swift Run Gap and Rosser to Swoope's, five miles west of Staunton.

Rosser's raid on Moorefield, New Creek and Piedmont, from which he had only recently returned, yielded great and unexpected results, for he had captured and destroyed vast quantities of army and railway material at both New Creek (Keyser) and Piedmont, besides 8 pieces of artillery, part of which he brought off. Also about 350 prisoners, and all with very small loss to his own troops. The capture of the forts at New Creek on the 28th of November, being a complete surprise in broad daylight, was a disgrace to the garrison. At Piedmont, on the Baltimore and Ohio Railroad, five miles west of New Creek, a detachment, under Major McDonald, endeavored to destroy the railway material and shops, but succeeded only partially in so doing, being prevented by the small garrison of Federal troops, thirty-five men in all, under Captain Fisher of the Sixth West Virginia Infantry.

Rosser then hurriedly withdrew his division to New Market by the route he had come, via Greenland Gap, Petersburg and Brock's Gap, rejoining Early in the upper valley.

For permitting his garrison at New Creek to be surprised, and the consequent humiliating losses of prisoners and public stores, Colonel Latham, Fifth West Virginia Cavalry, the commander, was sentenced by court-martial to be dismissed from the service, but this sentence was subsequently revoked by a War Department order and Colonel Latham was "honorably mustered out of the service at his own request March 9, 1865."

On the 28th of November, 1864, after Early had withdrawn to the region of Staunton in the upper valley,

General Sheridan, from his intrenched camp at Kernstown, sent out Merritt's Division of cavalry to clear the country of guerrillas east of the Blue Ridge and in Loudoun county. This was the main field of operations of the Confederate partisan Colonel Mosby, who had shown much enterprise in capturing small bodies of Federal troops passing through the country, both east and west of the Blue Ridge, attacking parties repairing railroads, or insufficiently guarded wagon-trains, and for which he had received the warmest approval of General Lee.

Sheridan, in his report of the Valley campaign, mentions the annoyance these guerrillas or partisan bands had caused him, but had constantly refused to operate against them, "believing them to be, substantially, a benefit to me, as they prevented straggling and kept my trains well closed up, and discharged such other duties as would have required a provost-guard of at least two regiments of cavalry." In retaliation for the assistance and sympathy given them, however, by the inhabitants of Loudoun valley, Sheridan sent out Merritt, with instructions to operate in the region east of the Blue Ridge "bounded on the south by the Manassas Gap Railroad as far east as White Plains, on the east by the Bull Run Range, on the west by the Shenandoah River, and on the north by the Potomac."

Merritt was further instructed to "consume and destroy all forage and subsistence, burn all barns and mills and their contents, and drive off all stock in the region. This order must be literally executed, bearing in mind, however, that no dwellings are to be burned, and that no personal violence be offered the citizens. The ultimate results of the guerrilla system of warfare are the destruction of all private rights in the country occupied by such parties. This destruction may as well commence at once, and the responsibility of it must rest upon the authorities at Richmond, who have acknowledged the legitimacy of guerrilla bands."

Merritt, in his report of December 6, 1864, says these orders "were most fully carried out," but although the entire Loudoun Region was gone over, few guerrillas were found.

Shortly after Merritt's return from Loudoun valley, Sheridan sent Custer's Cavalry Division up the Shenandoah to locate the whereabouts of Early's army. Custer left the vicinity of Kernstown at an early hour on the 19th of December, by way of the Valley Turnpike. At Woodstock, on the 20th, Custer first learned of the presence of the Confederate cavalry advanced scouts, who were picketing the three roads leading down the Valley—the turnpike, the Middle and the Back roads—extending from Edenburg westward to Little North Mountain. Custer took with him but three days' rations and one day's forage, expecting to find the enemy's cavalry no farther south than New Market; but finding no serious opposition even at Woodstock, and learning of no large force of the enemy being nearer than Staunton, Custer continued his march into the region that had been devastated by General Grant's orders in the early autumn, camping at

Lacey's Springs, 9 miles north of Harrisonburg, during the night of December 20. Strong pickets were thrown out toward Harrisonburg in front, Keezletown on the left, Timberville on the right, and a large force was left on the pike well to the rear.

In this position Custer was attacked about 6 A. M. of the 21st by Payne's Brigade of Rosser's Cavalry Division from the direction of Timberville, to Custer's right and rear, toward which point they had marched from their camp near Staunton the day before, reaching Custer's vicinity during the night of December 20. Rosser's other two brigades attacked from the back road.

These were all readily repulsed before daylight, after which there was no further demonstration, but as two of his three day's rations and all of his forage had been consumed, with no expectation of replenishing either for at least two days should he continue his advance to Staunton through a devastated country, Custer decided to retire, especially as the weather was exceedingly inclement and he had quite a number of wounded, mainly from sabre cuts, to care for. He took 32 prisoners, but does not state how many he lost in killed or captured, although Early claims Rosser took forty.

As Rosser attacked with sabres a force he expected to surprise in camp, but which he found on the alert, and who resisted with carbines at very short range, the probabilities are Rosser's losses in killed and wounded were larger than he cared to report.

Simultaneously with Custer's reconnaissance up the Valley to locate Early's army, General Sheridan sent another expedition of two divisions of cavalry under Torbert, to proceed from Winchester across the Blue Ridge by way of Front Royal and Chester Gap, thence south, to carry out, if practicable, General Grant's favorite hobby of seizing Gordonsville and Charlottesville, with a view to destroying the Virginia Central Railroad at those points.

Torbert's column moved out the same day as Custer's (December 19), both columns suffering intensely from the severe winter weather. By the morning of the 20th Early had already received information of the movements of both commands, and prepared to meet them from both sides of the Blue Ridge with his greatly depleted and much scattered forces, together with such reinforcements as could be sent him from Richmond by rail.

At that time Early had already sent off to Lee three of his divisions of infantry and, with his one remaining infantry division (Wharton's), had established his winter quarters at Fishersville, on the Central Railroad, a few miles west of Waynesboro. He had placed one of his cavalry divisions (Rosser's) at Swoope's, five miles west of Staunton, while Lomax's Cavalry Division was posted east of the Blue Ridge, between Gordonsville and Liberty Mills. All these points were easily reached by rail and were outside the zone of Sheridan's destructive autumn operations.

When Sheridan had learned earlier in the month that Early had sent away Kershaw's, Gordon's and Pegram's Divisions, he, too, detached all of the Sixth Corps (Wright's) and sent it to Grant at Petersburg, by way of Harper's Ferry, Washington, Chesapeake bay and City Point. In addition he sent Grant one division of Crook's Eighth Army Corps, withdrawing the remainder of that corps to Cumberland, where it went into winter quarters.

This left to Sheridan for immediate service in the Valley, the two divisions of the Nineteenth Corps (Emory's) and Torbert's three divisions of cavalry, and he had placed the railroad from Harper's Ferry in running order almost to his camps around Winchester.

The two divisions of the Nineteenth Army Corps were also subsequently withdrawn and sent to Grant.

Torbert approached Gordonsville by way of Madison Court-House, driving in Jackson's Brigade of Lomax's cavalry, which rallied at Liberty Mills, and, together with McCausland's Brigade, succeeded in delaying Torbert there by destroying the bridge over the Rapidan and forcing Torbert to use the fords both above and below, when Lomax's troopers hastily fell back to a line of defenses immediately north of Gordonsville, which Torbert assaulted but could not carry, early on the morning of the 23rd. He had succeeded the night before, however, in capturing two field pieces and some thirty prisoners, with small losses.

Having failed to dislodge Lomax, Torbert endeavored to flank him out by sending a strong column to turn the left of the position. While that movement was proceeding, the cars came in from Richmond loaded with infantry, which soon after were seen to file into the works. Torbert then became convinced it was useless further to attempt to break the Virginia Central Railroad at that point, and withdrew via Madison Court-House, with a loss of "six or eight men killed and about forty wounded, more than I could transport, and the worst cases were left behind. About thirty prisoners were taken, but having no provisions, and it being very difficult, if not impossible for them to keep up, I paroled them. The guns, two three-inch rifles, were brought to camp."

The infantry which Torbert saw file into the entrenchments in South West Mountain, north of Gordonsville, was Bratton's Brigade of Field's Division, which had been taken out of the lines in front of Petersburg and hurriedly sent by rail to Gordonsville at Early's call for assistance; Hunton's Brigade was following Bratton's, but did not reach Gordonsville when Torbert withdrew. The alarm being over, Hunton and Bratton were as rapidly taken back as they had been taken away from the lines of Lee's army.

With the return of Torbert's expedition to Sheridan's army at Winchester, operations in the Valley or in the adjacent region were suspended.

EPILOGUE

Sheridan devoted the months of January and February, 1865, to the refitting of his cavalry and light artillery in the vicinity of Winchester, preparing for a renewal of his campaign against Early.

On the 31st day of December, 1864, Early's strength in the region of Fishersville and Staunton, as shown by his inspection reports, aggregated 3,611 men present and absent, with 28 guns. This strength was greatly diminished when the campaign against him opened two months later.

Both armies sent out small expeditions during January and February, noticeably one from Early's army, consisting of Rosser's cavalry, which went in January from their winter cantonment at Swoope's, a few miles west of Staunton, over the main Allegheny and Cheat River Mountains into Tygart's River Valley, and surprised Beverly. In going, Rosser followed the old Parkersburg turnpike, one of the few good roads leading west and northwest out of the Valley, and had always been in coaching days, before the era of railroads, a favorite route to the Ohio River from Southern Virginia. It is in excellent order today and was driven over by the writer in August, 1902. Some of the old taverns of the days of 1860 still exist. Rosser, after capturing Beverly on the 11th of January, returned to Swoope's by way of Huntersville and Warm Springs.

The results of this raid were the capture of 572 officers and men belonging to the Eighth Ohio Cavalry and Thirty-fourth Ohio Infantry, about 100 horses, a small amount of quartermaster's stores and 10,000 rations, besides over 600 arms and equipments. The surprise was complete, as no attack was expected in the dead of winter, when the snows and inclement weather, as well as the isolation of the position among the mountains of West Virginia, gave a temporary fancied security to the garrison. The commanding officers of the Eighth Ohio Cavalry and Thirty-fourth Ohio Infantry were recommended for dismissal by General Crook, the Department Commander, "for disgraceful neglect."

As at the surprise and capture of New Creek November 28, 1864, three months before, Rosser's men wore Federal clothing, enabling them to effect a close approach before their identity could be discovered. Rosser claimed to have had only 300 men with him. If so, his division had dwindled away to the size of a diminutive regiment.

During January and February several cavalry expeditions were sent out from Sheridan's position at Winchester, mainly to operate against Mosby and White, east of the Blue Ridge, and against Harry Gilmor or the McNeills in the vicinity of Moorefield, to the westward in the South Branch of the Potomac Valley.

In one of these latter Harry Gilmor was surprised in bed at Randolph's, three miles out from Moorefield, at an early hour of the 5th of February. Gilmor, who appeared to be a freelance partisan from Maryland, had been sent by Early to take charge of the McNeill and Harness bands, operating near Moorefield, who resisted all control by anybody (especially by Gilmor).

Sheridan in his "Memoirs" says of Gilmor's capture: "Thus the last link between Maryland and the Confederacy was carried a prisoner to Winchester, whence he was sent to Fort Warren." The capture was effected by Colonel Young and twenty men of Sheridan's scouts, dressed in Confederate uniforms, supported by a mixed cavalry detachment of 300 men under Lieut.-Col. E. W. Whitaker, First Connecticut Cavalry. As an offset to this capture of Gilmor, a party of 50 of his men, led by young Jesse McNeill[xvi] and dressed in Federal uniforms, entered the City of Cumberland during the night of the 21st of February, proceeded direct to the hotel which was the headquarters of both Generals Kelley and Crook, surprising them in bed. Not a shot was fired and so little disturbance created, that staff officers living in rooms adjoining those of Generals Crook and Kelley, were not awakened.

The raiders remained only ten minutes in the town, and then hastily withdrew on the Springfield and Romney road with their prisoners, reaching Staunton in the upper Shenandoah on the 24th—all efforts to intercept the party having failed.

These captures were even more daringly made than was that of Harry Gilmor, about a fortnight earlier in the month, by Colonel Young.

On the 27th of February, 1865, Sheridan started from Winchester with two divisions of cavalry (Custer's and Devin's) and three sections of artillery, the whole commanded by Major-General Wesley Merritt.[xvii] The strength of the force was 9,987 officers and men.

The men carried five days' rations in haversacks, with fifteen days' additional rations of coffee, sugar and salt in wagons, thirty pounds of forage for each horse, one wagon for each division headquarters, eight ambulances and an ammunition train. No other wagons were allowed except a pontoon train of eight boats.

According to the instructions of General Grant, Sheridan was to destroy the Virginia Central Railroad, the James River canal, capture Lynchburg, if practicable, and then join General Sherman wherever he might be found in North Carolina, or return to Winchester.

Sheridan's troops were in fine condition for the movement, notwithstanding the bad condition of the roads and the continued inclemency of the weather, Early's depleted command near Staunton promising little opposition.

Staunton was reached in four marches and found abandoned by the enemy, who had withdrawn eastward to Waynesboro. He was closely followed and assaulted in position by Custer's Division, March 2d, who charged around and over the breastworks of Early's two brigades of infantry, dispersing them as well as a small body of cavalry under Rosser. The pursuit of the fugitives was continued as far as the South Fork of the Shenandoah River, where 11 pieces of artillery, with horses and caissons complete, 200 loaded wagons, 17 battle flags and 1,400 officers and men were captured. Generals Early, Long, Wharton, Lilley and Rosser, with a few men, escaped.

From Waynesboro the prisoners and captured artillery were sent back to Winchester under escort of 1,600 men, who safely reached their destination, although constantly harassed by a considerable force which Rosser had succeeded in gathering.

Meanwhile Custer pushed on to Charlottesville, destroying much government property on the way, besides the railroad and its bridges. At 4 p. m. of the 3d of March he was met by the mayor and prominent citizens of Charlottesville, that town so long coveted by General Grant, who surrendered the place peaceably.

Wharton, who had gathered a few of his infantry at Charlottesville the day before Custer's arrival, endeavored to find Early, but the latter with a small party had fled eastward toward Richmond.

With this dispersal of Early's army at Waynesboro, campaigns in the Shenandoah were ended.

Some minor scouting expeditions against Mosby's partisans were made from the region of Winchester, where Sheridan had left behind two or three thousand men to protect the lower valley. The line of the Baltimore and Ohio Railroad and of the Potomac River, from Harper's Ferry westward, were strongly held against possible raiding parties coming either from the direction of the country where Mosby continued to operate, or from the region of Moorefield, where Jesse McNeill still had a small following.

When Sheridan moved south from Winchester, President Lincoln showed some concern that Washington might be uncovered from that direction, but he was reassured by General Grant, who sent Hancock to command, during Sheridan's absence, all the territory comprised within the Middle Military Division, from Washington west to the Ohio River. Hancock's headquarters were fixed at Cumberland.

From Charlottesville Sheridan subsequently moved to the White House on the Pamunkey, and thence to the south side of the James, where he joined Grant and was placed by him on the extreme left of his army. That part of his instructions to capture Lynchburg and then strike out to join Sherman's army coming north through North Carolina, Sheridan found to be impracticable, on account of the very high stage of water in the James from Lynchburg down, all bridges having been destroyed and his eight pontoons being insufficient to effect a crossing.

NOTES

[i] Kenton Harper (1801 –1867) was an American printer, soldier, town mayor, banker, newspaper editor, and legislator. He served as an officer in the U.S. Army during the Mexican–American War and later as a Confederate general officer. Harper was purportedly credited with calling the attention of Brig. Gen. Bernard E. Bee to Stonewall Jackson's performance during the First Battle of Bull Run, inspiring Jackson's famous moniker.

[ii] "The tactical infantry unit of the Civil War, the brigade usually was made up of 4-6 regiments. However, it could have as few as 2 and later in the war, when consolidation of Confederate regiments became common, some brigades contained remnants of as many as 15 regiments. There were 3 or 4 brigades to a division and several divisions to a Corps. By definition, a brigadier general commanded a brigade. But colonels were often in charge of brigades too small to justify a brigadier, and if the brigadier was absent, the senior colonel would act in his stead; on occasion, temporary brigades organized for special purposes were commanded by colonels. The brigade's staff usually comprised the brigadier general, his aide, the quartermaster, ordnance and commissary officers, and inspector, and one or more clerks. The brigade's effectiveness depended on regimental and company commanders instructing their 1,000-1,500 men in the complicated maneuvers of the period, and on each regiment coordinating its movements with the others under the brigade commander. A poor commander might watch his brigade's actions dissolve into regimental or company-level conflicts coordinated loose, if at all, by the brigadier. Confederate brigades were known by the names of their commanders or former commanders; a much less prosaic system than that of the Federals, but a very confusing one. For example, the unit of "Pickett's Charge" at Gettysburg shown in Steele's *American Campaigns* as "McGowan's Brigade" was commanded by Pettigrew until 1 July '62 and then by Marshall. In this attack Pettigrew is commanding "Heth's Division," Trimble is commanding "Pender's Division," Mayo is commanding "Brockenbrough's Brigade," Marshall is commanding "McGowan's" or "Pettigrew's Brigade," Fry is commanding "Archer's Brigade," and Lowrance is commanding "Scales's Brigade."Some of the brigades became famous during the war. The Stonewall Brigade was one of Gen. R.E. Lee's best units, as was

Hood's Texas Brigade. Western Confederate brigades included the Orphan Brigade of Kentucky and the 1st Missouri Brigade. On the Union side, the Iron Brigade earned fame in the Army of the Potomac, as did the Philadelphia Brigade. Wilder's Lightning Brigade of mounted infantry combined infantry and cavalry tactics to become one of the best Union units." http://www.civilwarhome.com/armyorganization.htm Accessed December 13, 2013.

[iii] President Jefferson Davis appointed Leroy Pope Walker as the first Confederate Secretary of War. Walker's first major role involved the situation at Fort Sumter. His stint as Secretary of War was marked clashes with Jefferson Davis. His lack of experience in the military field hampered his ability to manage the war effort. In the wake of the "failure" of the Confederate army to pursue fleeing troops after the First Battle of Bull Run, the Davis administration received much criticism, and Walker began to be criticized even more. Walker resigned in September 1861. Davis named Judah P. Benjamin acting Secretary of War the same September, and he was confirmed in November 1861.

[iv] Col. George Deas was a military officer in the United States and Confederate Armies. He enlisted into the 5th United States Infantry on August 1, 1833 at the rank of 2nd Lieutenant. He received the honorary rank of Brevet Major, United States Army, for his actions at Contreras and Churubusco during the war with Mexico. He resigned his commission from the United States military on February 25, 1861 to cast his lot to the Confederacy. Within its army, he held the rank of Lieutenant Colonel serving as Inspector General. He also had assignments on the staffs of several Confederate Generals including the two highest ranking, Samuel Cooper and Robert E. Lee. In October 1862, he became the acting Assistant Secretary of War for the Confederacy. Confederate Lt. General James Longstreet was his brother-in-law. http://www.findagrave.com

[v] The Battle of Ball's Bluff, also known as the Battle of Harrison's Island or the Battle of Leesburg, was fought on October 21, 1861, in Loudoun County, Virginia, as part of Union Maj. Gen. George B. McClellan's operations in Northern Virginia. While a minor battle in comparison with those later to be fought, it was the second largest battle of the Eastern Theater in 1861, and in its aftermath had repercussions in the Union Army's chain of com-

mand structure and raised separation of powers issues under the United States Constitution during the war.

vi Robert Huston Milroy (1816 –1890) was a lawyer, judge, and a Union Army general in the American Civil War, most noted for his defeat at the Second Battle of Winchester in 1863. On May 8–9, 1862, Milroy led Union forces in the Battle of McDowell against Maj. Gen. Thomas J. "Stonewall" Jackson. Milroy's "spoiling attack" did not drive the Confederates from their position. The nadir of Milroy's military career was during the early days of the Gettysburg Campaign. He commanded the 2nd Division of the VIII Corps, Middle Department, from February 1863 until June. At the Second Battle of Winchester, he was outmaneuvered and "gobbled up" by the Confederate corps of Lt. Gen. Richard S. Ewell. He had been ordered to withdraw his 6,900-man garrison from Winchester, but he elected to remain in the face of the Confederate invasion, assuming that the fortifications of Winchester would withstand any assault or siege. On June 15, 1863, Milroy fled with his staff, but over 3,000 of his men were captured, as were all of his artillery pieces and 300 supply wagons. He was called before a court of inquiry to answer for his actions, but after ten months he was relieved of any liability for the catastrophe. He was then sent to the western theater of the war.

vii By twilight, Johnson's advance regiments reached Shaw's Fork, where they encamped. Because of the narrow roads and few camp sites, Jackson's army was stretched 8–10 miles back along the pike with its rear guard at Dry Branch Gap. Jackson made his headquarters at Rodgers's tollgate. During the night, Milroy withdrew behind the Bull Pasture River to McDowell, establishing headquarters in the Hull House.

viii Mechum's River Station no longer exists as a rail stop. Here Jackson's troops got on the train to Staunton on their way to McDowell in May of 1862. Also, this is where Jackson boarded a special train and headed east in late June of 1862. He would meet Lee and they would plan what was to become the Seven Days' Campaign.

ix At the eruption of the War Between the States, Lincoln appointed Banks as one of the first 'political' major generals, over the heads of West Point regulars, who resented him. A political general was usually a northern Democrat who Lincoln awarded with a generalship for loyalty to the Union. After the anguish of an humiliating defeat in the Shenandoah at the hands of the just now famous 'Stonewall' Jackson, Banks was sent to New Orleans to replace Benjamin Butler as commander of the Department of the Gulf, given the task of liberating the Mississippi. But Banks botched the reinforcement of Grant at Vicksburg, and only took the surrender of Port Hudson after Vicksburg had fallen, making further resistance futile. Banks was subsequently sent to the Red River campaign, a hopeless effort to occupy eastern Texas. Banks had no confidence in this stratagem, but the departing General-in-Chief, Henry Halleck, is said to have told Grant that it was Banks' idea, in order to get out of the responsibility for this expensive fiasco, which resulted in Banks finally being removed from command.

[x] Franz Sigel (1824 –1902) was a German military officer, a socialist revolutionist and immigrant to the United States who was a teacher, newspaperman, politician, and served as a Union major general in the American Civil War. Many Germans who were socialist or Marxist Revolutionaries fled their failed revolutions of 1848, and were thus known as the "48-ers". Believing in a highly centralized government, naturally they would join the Union army. A good book to read for more information on these people is *Red Republicans and Lincoln's Marxists: Marxism in the Civil War*, by Walter Kennedy and Al Benson. Of course not all Germans who fought in the War Between the States were Marxists. Nobleman Heros Von Borcke was a Major in Gen. JEB Stuart's cavalry. Jacob Gauss was a young bugler for Nathan Bedford Forrest, and a great favorite of his, to mention a few.

[xi] Sigel opened the Valley Campaigns of 1864, launching an invasion of the Shenandoah Valley. He was badly whipped by Maj. Gen. John C. Breckenridge at the Battle of New Market, on May 15, 1864, which was proved to be very embarrassing due to the prominent role young cadets from the Virginia Military Institute played in his defeat. After the battle, Sigel was replaced by Maj. Gen. David Hunter. In July, Sigel fought Lt. Gen. Jubal A. Early at Harpers Ferry, but soon afterward was replaced by Albion P. Howe. Sigel spent the rest of the war without an active command.

xii John Reese Kenly (1818-1891) of Baltimore, MD, was a Union army officer (Brigadier General). He entered the War Between the States as colonel of the 1st Regiment Maryland Volunteer Infantry organized at Baltimore, Maryland and mustered into Union service on May 16, 1861, which, together with some Pennsylvania companies, was captured by Stonewall Jackson, after fierce fighting, at Front Royal on the Shenandoah, May 23, 1862. Kenly was seriously wounded when he was taken prisoner, but his stand had saved General Banks's division at Winchester. For this, he was given command of a brigade later in 1862 after his recovery.

xiii There were two Fitzhugh Lees serving in Stuart's cavalry. They were first cousins. William Henry Fitzhugh Lee was known as "Rooney" and was the son of Robert E. Lee. Fitzhugh Lee was the son of Robert E. Lee's brother, Smith Lee (a naval commander) and was known as "Fitz" Lee.

xiv John Daniel Imboden (1823 –1895) was a native of Staunton, Virginia. He attended Washington College in Lexington and became a lawyer, teacher, and Virginia state legislator. During the War Between the States, he was a Confederate cavalry general and partisan fighter. After the war he returned to practicing law, began writing, and also was active in developing natural resources.

xv McCausland was born in St. Louis, Missouri on September 13, 1836, the son of an immigrant from Ireland. He became an orphan in 1843 and went to live with relatives near Point Pleasant, Virginia, now in Mason County, West Virginia. He graduated with honors in the class of 1857 at the Virginia Military Institute (VMI). In 1858, after graduating from the University of Virginia, McCausland became an assistant professor of mathematics at VMI until 1861. In 1859 he was present with a group of VMI cadets at the execution of John Brown at Charles Town. He died in 1927 at the age of 90.

xvi Jessie was the son of John McNeill. Legend portrays every man of the McNeill Rangers as a hero. Undoubtedly these Confederate guerrillas frequently struck terror into the hearts of Federal commanders by their sudden visitations, often made in the deep of night. Sustaining many casualties, they suffered more than the regulars of either the Confederate or Federal army since

their medical supplies were extremely meager. They endured innumerable hardships, but constant in their devotion to their political and social philosophy, they fought for the Confederate cause to the last.
http://www.wvculture.org/history/journal_wvh/wvh12-1.html

[xvii] A West Pointer, class of 1860, Wesley Merritt in early May 1863, rode with Cavalry Corps during Stoneman Raid. Designed as a deep penetration raid to support Major General Joseph Hooker's efforts at the Battle of Chancellorsville, the operation proved a failure. After the raid, Merritt was promoted to command the 2nd Cavalry which was then part of Brigadier General John Buford's Reserve Brigade. Because of this failure, Stoneman was removed and the Cavalry Corps given to Major General Alfred Pleasonton.

Made in the USA
Lexington, KY
04 March 2014